The Closure of
Mental Hospitals

Edited by
PETER HALL
IAN F. BROCKINGTON

The Closure of Mental Hospitals

GASKELL

ISBN 0 902241 35 4

Gaskell is an imprint of the Royal College of Psychiatrists,
17 Belgrave Square, London SW1

Distributed in North America
by American Psychiatric Press, Inc.
ISBN 0 88048 602 3

A CIP catalogue record for this book is
available from the British Library

Publication of this book was made
possible by the kind support of
Dista Products Limited

Phototypeset by Dobbie Typesetting Limited, Tavistock, Devon
Printed in Great Britain by
Henry Ling Limited, Dorchester, Dorset

Contents

Part III. Home treatment

Part IV. Appendix

List of contributors

Mr Charles Barker, Quality Assurance Manager (Mental Health Unit), Worcester and District Health Authority, Worcester

Dr David Battin, Consultant Psychiatrist for the Elderly, Worcester and District Health Authority, Worcester

Dr James L. T. Birley, formerly President, Royal College of Psychiatrists, London

Professor Ian F. Brockington, Professor of Psychiatry, University of Birmingham, Birmingham

Dr Patrick G. Campbell, Consultant Psychiatrist, Friern Hospital, Friern Barnet Road, New Southgate, London

Mr A. Neil Chapman, District Treasurer, Worcester and District Health Authority, Worcester

Dr Joseph Connolly, Consultant Psychiatrist, The Maudsley Hospital, London

Dr Christine Dean, Senior Lecturer in Psychiatry and Honorary Consultant, Queen Elizabeth Hospital, University of Birmingham, Birmingham

Dr Donald H. Dick, Consultant Psychiatrist, Herrison Hospital, Herrison, Dorchester

Dr Ian R. H. Falloon, Community Physician (Mental Health), Buckingham Health Service, Buckingham Hospital, Buckingham

Mr Raymond Gillard, Acute Unit General Manager, Worcester Royal Infirmary, Worcester

Mr Victor Graham-Hole, Director of Training, Buckingham Mental Health Service, Buckingham

Dr Peter Hall, Consultant Psychiatrist, Malvern Hills, Worcester Royal Infirmary, Newtown Branch, Worcester, and Adviser, Post-graduate Psychiatry, University of Birmingham

Dr Christine Hassall, Senior Research Fellow, Department of Psychiatry, University of Birmingham, Birmingham

Mr Simon Hodgson, Mental Health Unit General Manager, Worcester Royal Infirmary, Newtown Branch, Worcester

Dr John Hoult, Regional Mental Health Consultant, PO Box 160, Rozelle 2039, New South Wales, Australia

Mr John Jenkins, formerly Unit General Manager, Torbay Hospital, Lawes Bridge, Torquay, Devon

Dr Eric Jones, Bewdley, Worcestershire

Dr Deenesh Khoosal, Consultant Psychiatrist, Leicester Health Authority, Leicester

Dr Robin E. Lawrence, formerly Senior Registrar, Department of Psychiatry, The London Hospital, Whitechapel, London

Professor Julian P. Leff, Director, MRC Social Psychiatry Unit, Friern Hospital, Friern Barnett Road, London

Professor Isaac M. Marks, Professor of Experimental Psychopathology, Institute of Psychiatry, De Crespigny Park, London

Dr George Milner, Consultant Psychiatrist, Worcester Royal Infirmary, Newtown Branch, Worcester

Dr Wendy Morris, Research Associate, Department of Psychiatry, University of Birmingham

Dr Matthijs Muijen, Honorary Senior Registrar, Department of Psychiatry, The Maudsley Hospital, Denmark Hill, London

Mr Roger Powell, Planning Officer, Worcester and District Health Authority, Worcester

Mr Anthony Prescott, The Chairman, Worcester and District Health Authority, Worcester

Dr John Reed, Senior Principal Medical Officer, Department of Health, London

Dr Huw Richards, Consultant Psychiatrist, Worcester and District Health Authority, Worcester

Dr James A. Robertson, Consultant Psychiatrist, Department of Psychiatry, Kidderminster General Hospital, Kidderminster, Worcestershire

Dr Norman Sartorius, Director, Division of Mental Health, World Health Organization, Geneva, Switzerland

Professor C. Philip Seager, Director, Health Advisory Service, London, Professor of Psychiatry, University Department, Northern General Hospital, Sheffield

Mr Michael Spicer, Member of Parliament for South Worcestershire, House of Commons, London

Dr Robin Steel, General Practitioner, Worcester

Professor Leonard Stein, Professor of Psychiatry, University of Wisconsin, Madison, Wisconsin, USA

Mr David Tombs, Director of Social Services, Hereford and Worcester County Council, Worcester

Mr James C. Waits, District General Manager, Worcester and District Health Authority, Worcester

Ms Judy Weleminsky, Director of the National Schizophrenia Fellowship, London

Professor John K. Wing, CBE, formerly Director, MRC Social Psychiatry Unit, Institute of Psychiatry, London, now Director, Royal College of Psychiatrists Research Unit, London

Dr Stephen Wood, formerly Consultant Psychiatrist, Guy's Hospital, London

Foreword by the Chairman of Worcester and District Health Authority

ANTHONY PRESCOTT

We were delighted as a district health authority to welcome delegates from Australia, the USA, Canada, Switzerland, Greece, Denmark, Norway, Holland, Sweden and Ireland (as well as from all over the UK) to the Malvern Symposium, of which this book is a record. We were encouraged to feel that this underlined the relevance of our activities in this field over recent years and were aware that the government paper of 1975 – ''Better Services for the Mentally Ill'' – had drawn heavily on our experience in the Worcester Development Project. We were also very pleased to co-promote this meeting with the University of Birmingham, and honoured by the joint sponsorship of the World Psychiatric Association and the World Federation of Mental Health, as well as by the selection of the Malvern service by the World Health Organization to be one of its field research centres. The Director of the Mental Health Division of the World Health Organization, the President and Secretary-General of the World Psychiatric Association, the President of the Royal College of Psychiatrists and the ex-President of the World Federation of Mental Health all attended the meeting in person – a considerable and appreciated honour.

Worcester has often been in the vanguard of psychiatric care, particularly since its burghers built Powick Pauper Lunatic Asylum in 1845. This hospital attracted Sir Edward Elgar as its first bandmaster and the bandstand in which he conducted concerts still stands within the hospital grounds.

Powick's more modern renaissance began with the appointment of the late Dr Arthur Spencer as medical superintendent and Dr Ronald Sandison as his deputy in the early 1950s, and in 1963 the joint appointment of a consultant between the hospital and the University of Birmingham. Since that time, there has been close co-operation between Worcester and successive professors of psychiatry, and indeed Professor Sir William Trethowan chaired the Worcester Development Project Coordinating Committee in the 1960s.

In 1968, the government was prompted to establish a single national project to demonstrate the problems of transition from the old-style service to a new community-based form of service. Powick Hospital was chosen to be the test-bed, and thus was born the Worcester Development Project. It can be argued that the development of psychiatric services in Worcester would have taken place without the Development Project, but there is little doubt that this would not have happened as it did without the interest of the Department of Health and without direct funding to health authorities and local authorities, all of which greatly speeded up the process and made service changes more acceptable to these authorities as well as to the local community.

Powick Hospital near Malvern was the first large general psychiatric institution in Britain to be closed following the provision of major community-based replacement services, and St Wulstan's Hospital in Malvern probably the first mental illness hospital of any kind to close in the UK. Acute psychiatric services for this area are now being provided by Worcester Royal Infirmary together with day hospitals and a network of community-based psychiatric nurses. Hostels, flats, and group homes provide both independence and supervised living for long-stay patients, in a partnership between the local authority, the health authority, and housing associations. A modern industrial therapy workshop, personal social service, and voluntary day centres are also available as, since 1989, are three small units for the elderly mentally ill, which are geographically dispersed around the district. They provide the comfort and security required by these elderly vulnerable patients, many of whom have been institutionalised for 60 years and more, as well as a homely domestic environment. These units and several hostels are about to be handed over to the voluntary sector.

The 18th century saw Malvern on the spa map because of the Malvern Water Cure, and I am pleased that it is on the medical map again.

Foreword by the Member of Parliament for South Worcestershire

MICHAEL SPICER

My interest in the Malvern Symposium is very much that of a layman. I do not necessarily apologise for that, because I think that laymen are important in the whole question of what should be the future of mental health services in this country, and indeed in the world. I have been Member of Parliament for South Worcestershire for 15 years and have therefore been very much involved in some of the battles which have been waged and debates which have taken place about the closure of the institutions for the mentally ill in my constituency.

The big question before politicians in the 1970s was whether or not there was such a thing as 'rehabilitation'. There were then subsets of questions about whether or not rehabilitation could take place outside a hospital, the big issue being whether or not there were 'comparable facilities' to replace institutions. During that period, of course, the Worcester Development Project was beginning to evolve. In this part of the world, there was not only the closure of two major institutions, one of which had specialised in rehabilitation, but also the beginnings of a focused and coherent policy of care within the community. When institutions are closed, should the state really 'pick up the tab'? Should it do so in such a way as to be able to cope with the problems of people who had previously been cared for by means which – in some people's view – were not totally satisfactory, but which nevertheless appeared to be economical? One of the interesting questions that is emerging out of the Worcester experiment concerns the resources that are going to be required. Not only is it a question of the relative costs of different forms of care, but, and this is by far the most difficult and intractable question, which I could never really get a grip of as a politician, one of relative effectiveness. I do not know, as a layman, whether or not care within the community or outside large hospitals is more or less demanding of resources, though I suspect that this is capable of measurement. Much more difficult, I suspect, is the question of relative effectiveness.

Until the day arises when the medical profession can make us immortal, there will never be enough resources going into health care, almost by definition. Even if we spent our entire national budget on health, it would still be a reasonable argument to say that we should spend one pound more. The demand will always outstrip supply, so far as resources are concerned. Therefore, all those concerned in the provision of health, have, at various levels, to ration, to make choices. The government believes that the decisions about these choices should be made further down, by the professionals, and that is a controversial issue. At the end of the day, the choice has to be made by someone between how much resources are put into mental health, how much into other forms of health care, how much public money is put into things that have nothing to do with health at all. The choice will in part be made on grounds of cost-effectiveness. I shall continue to watch the Worcester experiment with great interest.

Editorial note and acknowledgements

PETER HALL and IAN F. BROCKINGTON

The Worcester Development Project opened in 1978 as the then Ministry of Health's national demonstration project of a comprehensive community-based psychiatric service. Although the large mental hospital in South Worcestershire ceased to take any new admissions as from 5 December 1978, it was not until 1989 that it closed completely.

The Department of Psychiatry at the University of Birmingham and the Worcester and District Health Authority took the opportunity of the closure of Powick Hospital in March 1989 to organise a major international psychiatric meeting in Malvern. It was felt by us that a report of the meeting might interest the numerous mental health clinical professionals and managers who are trying to develop similar, analogous or more advanced services, the more so since the government decision to follow the precedent of the Worcester Development Project that large psychiatric institutions should not close in future before satisfactory alternative facilities were available.

Because of considerations of space, the editors have unfortunately had to condense or omit a number of contributions to the symposium. It has been editorial policy to give preference to contributions by local 'naïve domestic burgundy', who have hard-earned experience to report and which might otherwise not have seen the light of published day.

First and foremost we are indebted to Dista Products Limited (Eli Lilly) for their generosity in supporting this publication. We are also grateful to several pharmaceutical companies for their valued support of the meeting itself – Boots Company PLC, Delandale Laboratories Limited, Dista Products Limited, Duphar Laboratories Limited, Hoechst UK Limited, Janssen Pharmaceutical Limited, Lundbeck Limited, E. Merck Limited, Organon Laboratories Limited, Schering Health Care Limited, and E. R. Squibb and Sons Limited – and also the Woodbourne Clinic, Birmingham. We very much appreciated the sponsorship of the World Psychiatric Association, the World Federation of Mental Health, the Worcester and District Health Authority, and the University of Birmingham.

We also most gratefully acknowledge the help of colleagues and staff too numerous to acknowledge individually, both in the Worcester and District Health Authority (particularly in its Mental Health Unit) and in the University Department of Psychiatry. The contributions of Mr Ray Gillard, attendees of Gregory's Mill Centre, of Mr David Birtwhistle, of Mr David Craven, of Universal Conference Consultants, of the Little Orchestra of Worcester, of Professor Hugh Freeman and the staff of the Publications Department at the Royal College of Psychiatrists, of Mike Cresswell and his staff at the Winter Gardens, Malvern, of Ms Karen Cunningham, of the Very Reverend Frank Bentley, of the Lord Mayor of Worcester, of the Chairman and Councillors of Malvern Council, and of many other colleagues and friends, particularly the Members of the Malvern Psychiatric and Social Services teams, were particularly appreciated. Our secretaries Jean Smith, Jane Radford, Wendy Schwab, and Penny Jolly were of enormous help not only in the preparation of manuscripts but also in the organisation of the meeting itself. Jenny Holmes in particular has patiently typed and reorganised several drafts of the manuscript.

Introduction

JAMES L. T. BIRLEY

This book records and celebrates the long and arduous process of replacing the services provided by a traditional mental hospital with a different network of treatment and care. This occurred in Worcestershire, England – a comparatively rural and settled area, but the range of problems and of solutions have been under active consideration all over the world. The Worcester experiment thus caught both national and international attention.

In April 1989, a symposium was held in Malvern to mark this important achievement in British psychiatry. The speakers included those involved locally and from further afield. Their contributions provide a 'state-of-the-art' account of current service developments.

The history of Powick Hospital, described so vividly by Dr Hall in Chapter 7, illustrates how much an institution's standard of care can depend, for better or worse, on one person – the medical superintendent. In a more open system, one person is less likely to hold so much power, but standards can and will vary considerably. The Worcester experiment should remain an object of evaluation for years to come, for the sake of its own citizens and for those living far beyond Worcester.

There will continue to be lively argument as to whether all the traditional functions of a mental hospital can be provided in the future pattern of service. At the end of two days of cautious optimism, the symposium held its own debate, recorded here, which ended with a majority voting in favour of the continued need for asylum.

I. The closure of mental hospitals

1 A European perspective on community care for the mentally ill

NORMAN SARTORIUS

The perspective presented in this chapter is personal; it does not rely on an international consensus about mental health care, because there is no such consensus nor any joint policy. There are countries which would be interested in formulating and using a set of mental health tenets to govern programme development – but they are not very numerous. There are also countries which would wish to formulate policies for others or support such policies, as long as they would not be obliged to use them in their own programmes. Finally, there are countries which are not convinced that there is any benefit for them in making up such principles, and would not accept them if they existed.

In the implementation of programmes, there are also differences, not only among countries but also between states in large federally structured countries. Programmes vary in their comprehensiveness, in their style, and in the type of resources they have or seek. In some countries, governments have undertaken in-depth studies of mental health problems, established parliamentary commissions, and reviewed legislation; in others, in spite of the significant number of people disabled and the major expenditures caused by mental disorders, there is no visibility for the mental health service programmes in the medium- or long-term plans for health care developed by their governments. Some countries restrict the scope of their mental health programmes to care of the most severely ill; others are more comprehensive and also pay appropriate attention to psychosocial aspects of health in general. Yet in spite of these differences, there are certain common trends in the development of mental health policies and programmes and certain principles that are becoming generally accepted.

Awareness about the enormity of the problems, suffering, and economic loss related to psychiatric disorders has continued to grow worldwide. Psychosocial and behavioural factors are becoming recognised as determinants of the success of health-care programmes, of quality of life, and of overall national development efforts. Life-style and behaviour are increasingly seen as being central to the aetiology and control of disease. The fact that many psychiatric and neurological disorders can be avoided by the application of measures of primary prevention and that the vast majority of psychiatric disorders can be effectively treated in general health care has not yet become an accepted part of thinking about public health – but even here, progress has been visible over the past decade.

In Europe in particular, certain common trends have become clearly visible. In most of its countries, there is a trend towards a geographical decentralisation of highly specialised services, which increasingly often are being established in areas distant from the capital. Improved communications and transport to peripheral parts of the country, better schooling, and universal access to material (and cultural) goods have acted as powerful factors in the decisions of younger staff to move to services in the provinces. By and large, the quality of care has not decreased in the decentralised system, and a number of excellent peripheral services have sprung up in many countries. Sometimes such peripheral units coexist with traditional mental hospitals, and sometimes they have grown within them or have replaced them.

There has also been an extensive 'ideological' decentralisation of health care. While previously both an expectation of leadership and an acceptance of the principles of health care as stated by the central authority (with the technical blessing of the university department of psychiatry in the capital) were commonplace, the peripheral services in many European countries now reject this relationship with the capital and rely on their own expertise and technical authority.

A third form of decentralisation – from specialised psychiatric services to psychiatric units in general hospitals and institutions – has been much slower. For example, in the ten years from 1972 to 1981, the number of psychiatric units in general hospitals in Europe grew from 408 to 615 – a remarkable increase; yet the beds in these units now constitute only 10% of all beds for psychiatric patients, compared with a previous 6% (Freeman *et al*, 1985). The resources for in-patient care have thus remained where they were before, although the many innovations which have been attempted in mental health service organisations over the years would require a significant shift of resources.

Self-help movements have become an important factor in psychiatric care in Europe. Some of them are organisations of patients, such as Depressive Anonymous; others involve the relatives of schizophrenics or other types of patients. These self-help groups vary, but seem to fall neatly into three groups: those that act as an extension of the psychiatric service and abide by the rules and instructions given by that service; those that are established in opposition to the psychiatric service and actively militate against individual psychiatrists, the service, and the mental health profession as a whole; and finally, those that are independent but willing to negotiate with psychiatric services about various issues, while accepting some advice and guidance. Self-help movements flourish in the north; in the south of Europe they are much less well developed and are accepted only with reluctance.

In several European countries, the cost of mental health care has gone up so quickly (and so much) that drastic measures have been taken to stem further cost explosion. In some instances, it has been recommended that professional administrators become managers of psychiatric services at both community and district levels. In other countries, a significant amount of administrative control has been introduced, often entailing considerable expense, as well as causing delays and dissatisfaction within the service and in the population that it serves. Cost-reduction schemes are being tried out in a number of countries but their life is usually short and they often disappear or are replaced by new schemes, even before they have been fully assessed and described. The entry of chains of private hospitals into European countries has also contributed to the attention given to the economy of service provision and to the rationalisation of expenditures in the public sector. Economic considerations are also often at the basis of trends in the length of stay in hospitals, as well as in determining patterns of migration of health personnel within Europe.

A most welcome tendency in a number of European countries has been the growing emphasis on quality of care, which has taken on a variety of forms, ranging from peer review to the establishment of special inspectorates that monitor quality of care. Special committees (involving medical personnel and others) to control quality of patient care and multidisciplinary teams to analyse accidents in hospitals, for example, have come into existence, representing desirable innovations in the efforts to ensure a minimum standard of psychiatric care. The decrease in size of psychiatric facilities and the delegation of power to local authorities have both helped and hindered control of the quality of care in some countries: helped, because local authorities can be more familiar with the situation and more aware of both constraints and possibilities; hindered, because independence from the central authority also means that funds necessary to introduce innovations have to be found locally, by reducing some other activity financed by the peripheral authority. Furthermore, local authorities do not always see the necessity for research which was earlier carried out with 'central', common funds and it is not easy to deal with problems that are relatively rare in each of the localities but still concern a large number of people in the country as a whole (e.g. services for patients with a rare disease or with an unusual combination of needs).

Legislation concerning the treatment of the mentally ill and the promotion of mental health has been revised in a number of European countries (Mangen, 1985). In the new laws, there is more emphasis on the protection of patients' human rights and individual responsibility. However, a regrettable consequence of the concern about confidentiality of data about patients has been the disestablishment of several psychiatric registers in Europe (e.g. in the Federal Republic of Germany).

A variety of 'new' psychiatric services have come into existence, though some of them are more the consequence of the search for 'a place in the sun' by professionals, rather than a result of a rational analysis of patients' needs and of ways to satisfy them. Crisis intervention units, for example, have sprung up in a number of countries (Cooper, 1979). Recent analyses of such new services demonstrate that there are considerable differences in their structure and content of work: often, they are new only in name.

The use of alternative medicine and traditional healers of different types, from magnetisers and hand-layers to herbalists and astrologers, seems to be on the increase in most European countries, though exact figures about the total number of healers and about the number of patients visiting them are difficult to obtain. Anecdotal reports, however, indicate that the numbers of healers match or exceed the numbers of doctors trained in recognised medical schools. No doubt, the search for help from traditional 'healers' is at least in part driven by the growing dehumanisation of many services, in which technological solutions and numerous laboratory examinations largely suppress human contact and empathy. Many patients seem to use the services of practitioners of 'soft medicine' as well as of those trained in medical schools.

Differences in the style, duration, and content of both undergraduate and postgraduate training courses in psychiatry in Europe have, if anything, increased over the past two decades (López-Ibor & Lenz, 1984). The minimum training for psychiatrists and other mental health service staff differs widely. In some countries, there are no examinations for mental health workers while in others there are examinations for several degrees, which are extremely formalised. Such differences between countries have rendered exchange of staff, fellowship programmes, and similar activities increasingly difficult.

Recent years have seen the emergence of powerful interprofessional rivalries in the field of mental health. Psychologists have become much more numerous, contend for health funds, and request legislative procedures that would enable them to practise psychiatry and 'behavioural' medicine. Other professions have also grown in numbers, requesting independence and competing for their share in the treatment of disease. General practitioners and specialists in internal medicine who have had brief training in psychology or psychiatry, psychiatric social workers, defectologists, speech therapists, and a variety of other professions have increased in numbers; in contrast, psychiatric nursing has had a significant drop in the number of entrants. This is partly due to the decrease in the number of psychiatric hospitals (and thus posts), and partly to the increasing complexity and length of both basic and further nursing training, which make many candidates opt for medicine or other health professions with more prestige and remuneration than nursing.

A continuing problem on the European mental health scene is the lack of co-ordination between the various social-service sectors that are involved in the care for the mentally ill and impaired. In some countries, co-ordinating committees involving representatives of different sectors have been set up, with beneficial effects; in others, parliamentary commissions have been established to examine mental health care and recommend changes.

Most European countries, however, have not yet acted to reduce such overlap and to render activities of the different sectors more logical and coherent. Programmes for alcohol- and drug-related health problems and those for mental retardation illustrate this tendency particularly well. Although people with problems usually seek help from mental health services, planning and financing of treatment for these conditions have in some countries been taken out of the health system and passed to other ministries or organisations.

Therapeutic techniques in the field of mental health care have been exposed to serious scrutiny, and some (such as electroconvulsive therapy) are being used much less or not at all in certain countries. There has been a conscious and intensive effort to simplify treatment techniques and to make it possible for general practitioners and other health staff to deal with psychiatric disorders competently. Weekend courses on the management of depression (and similar training activities) for general practitioners enjoy considerable popularity. Numerous manuals and instructions on ways of dealing with a particular problem in oneself or in patients are being published and widely distributed among professionals and even among the lay public. The use and appeal of psychoanalysis are by and large on the decline, though there are major differences between countries in this respect.

All of the developments described above have to be seen in the framework of several more fundamental changes, affecting not only mental health programmes but health and development in general. The first of these is the change of structure of basic social units – the family and the community. After a period of decrease in family size and of its nuclearisation, many European countries are experiencing a renaissance of family cohesion, but in a new garb and in a redefined manner. Powerful communication technology – from roads and telephones to electronic mail – combined with increased incomes allowing its extensive use, have changed the sense of geographical distance and separation. Reunions of families have become easier and more popular, whilst immunity from family problems based on distance is a thing of the past. The previous forms of mutual support and joint resistance to misery have changed or disappeared, but new ones have come into existence.

The opposite has happened in relation to community. For a long time, the term 'community' has referred to a social unit sharing physical space or a geographical area, having links of barter, cultural exchange, and mutual support. The individuals living in a community were enmeshed in a network of relationships and obligations, often going back for generations. Urbanisation and the life-style required by current industrial and agricultural developments have changed the concept of the community to such an extent that it may not constitute a valid element in planning health care any longer. For large parts of Europe, communities are composed of individuals linked by professional, financial, and other relationships, rather than by sharing the same geographical area. Individuals and families living in residential areas of modern urban agglomerations are loosely connected with each other, and are unlikely to be willing or able to fulfil the roles which community members previously considered as inevitable for those sharing a given geographical space. The disappearance of the previous emotional and social closeness of those living next to each other has decreased the power and potential of local authorities, which earlier relied on their capacity to mobilise the relatively homogeneous groups contained in their communities for a common cause. Religious leaders have also changed their relationships with those living in the territory which they are supposed to cover. Generally, priests no longer know the family histories of members of their flock, and no longer call on their inherent authority for community action. More and more often, they change the register of their action, assuming advisory roles and spending much of their energy on attempts to establish social cohesion. Large numbers of migrant workers, often concentrated in limited areas, further affect the earlier definition of 'community' and its usefulness as a concept within a planning process that aims to produce rational and economically viable proposals for the care of the mentally ill.

The second fundamental change that recent decades have brought with them is a significant shift in the responsibility for health. The notion that the health services – and the government – are responsible for every aspect of the health of citizens has lost its power. There are still some tasks that are within the obligations of health services, for example regular examinations of school children and the issuance of standards to avoid air pollution dangerous to health. But increasingly, health services are abrogating their responsibility and tend to take the position that individuals and families must themselves take on tasks concerning their health and find ways to improve it. Individuals are supposed to seek ways to protect themselves from disease, control their health behaviour and diet, look after the health of those in their families, and accept the need to live a healthier but often more boring life. It is the individual's duty to visit a dentist at regular intervals, rather than the dentist's duty to invite citizens in for a check-up. The consequences of this change for mental health programmes are considerable, particularly when combined with trends of relative reduction of resources for long-term care and disability, regardless of cause.

A third change of a general nature that is likely to affect mental health programmes in Europe is a continuing and increasing shift of thresholds for impairment and disability. This is affected by a variety of factors: for example, by the pandemic growth of minor impairments due to better survival chances of those with an impairment, by growing life expectancy at all ages, by the increasing numbers of the elderly, by general education, by the changing distribution of labour, and by other factors inherent to today's socio-economic development and growth.

These three changes, as well as the common trends described, do not exhaust the list of factors profoundly affecting care for the mentally ill; they all contribute to the map in which we have to seek the best way to achieve progress – one that is suited to our needs and to our resources. It is important to do this together, with all those concerned – regardless of sector or profession – so as to make socio-economic development humane, and enable all of us – including those affected by mental illness – to live a life of quality.

References

COOPER, J. E. (1979) *Crisis Admission Units and Emergency Psychiatric Services.* Copenhagen: WHO, Regional Office for Europe.
FREEMAN, H. L., FRYERS, T. & HENDERSON, J. H. (1985) *Mental Health Services in Europe: 10 years on.* Copenhagen: WHO, Regional Office for Europe.
LÓPEZ-IBOR, J. J. & LENZ, G. (eds) (1984) *Training and Education in Psychiatry.* Vienna: Facultas.
MANGEN, S. P. (1985) *Mental Health Care in the European Community.* London: Croom Helm.

2 Vision and reality

JOHN K. WING

Vision

During the mid-1950s, the possibility began to be discussed that care for people disabled or disturbed by various kinds of mental illness or handicap could be provided without recourse to the large mental hospitals that were then the mainstay of the psychiatric services. Reform had already begun in some hospitals during the '30s but had been interrupted by the war. It began again in the late '40s, with the incorporation of all hospitals into one National Health Service, and the entry of a post-war generation of professional staff.

The peak of bed occupancy (after a more or less steady rise throughout the century) occurred in 1954. 'Run-down' began earlier in some hospitals but first became visible in the national statistics in 1955. It has continued ever since. This was not a 'top-down' policy decision but was due to the introduction of social methods of rehabilitation and resettlement by pioneering doctors, nurses and social workers, followed by the first really effective medications.

Closure plans began to be formulated in the late '50s and the issues involved were brought to wide public notice in 1961 by Enoch Powell, the then Minister of Health. He said:

> "Building hospitals is not like building pyramids, the erection of memorials to a remote posterity. We have to get it into our heads that a hospital is like a shell, a framework to contain certain processes, and when the processes are superseded, the shell must, most probably, be scrapped and the framework dismantled." (Powell, 1961)

That statement contained two messages. One was about 'processes' – a good sociological word that includes the functions of diagnosis, assessment, treatment, enabling, caring and the general promotion of welfare and quality of life. It therefore includes the functions of asylum (Wing, 1990a). The second was about the structure of services, including professional staff,

10

specialised day, residential and domiciliary facilities, and efficient organisation and management, all dedicated to the reduction of disability and the promotion of health.

By 1961, the processes were already changing and the outline of a new structure was already evident. Two-thirds of the residents were 'long stay', a term then meaning more than two years in hospital. Of these, two-thirds had a diagnosis of schizophrenia. If residents with this disorder could be decently resettled outside, and if new services could be set up to prevent further accumulation, much of the justification for large institutions would disappear. The question was, could the vision be turned into reality and would it work?

Looking back at that time, another question needs to be answered. What should be the standard for comparison? There were good and bad hospitals. Should we be content with doing better than the worst examples of authoritarian, custodial and deadening institutions? Or should we take as our standard the best practice of those times and judge progress against that?

Between 1960 and 1968, cross-sectional studies were made of women in three mental hospitals, all suffering from schizophrenia, aged under 60, and resident for more than two years (Wing & Brown, 1970). Among those who had stayed between two and five years, more than three-quarters wanted to leave. (An earlier study had shown that, very shortly after admission, nearly all people with schizophrenia wanted to leave.) With increasing periods of residence, more and more appeared indifferent or actually wanted to stay. Other measures showed that social withdrawal, poor contact with the outside, few personal possessions, and unfavourable attitudes of nurses, were all related to length of stay.

The results were not uniform across the three hospitals. R. K. Freudenberg and his colleagues had created at Netherne Hospital (Coulsdon, Surrey) a rehabilitation service with outreach into the community that had achieved an international reputation. On most variables the results at Netherne were highly favourable compared with those at Severalls (Colchester), which was at the other end of the spectrum. Mapperley Hospital (Nottingham) came between, with some of the characteristics of Netherne and some of those of Severalls. When the reforms introduced at Severalls by Russell Barton took effect, the results there became much more favourable.

This research was concerned with different models of treatment, enabling and care, though all were implemented within the same kind of hospital 'shell'. A second example from the same period provides a comparison between an early version of community care and more traditional models (Brown *et al*, 1966). This was a study of patients with schizophrenia who were admitted to the same three hospitals in 1956 and followed up five years later. Many of the community-care ideas now taken for granted were first put into practice in Nottingham by Duncan Macmillan, who before the war had been the city's medical officer for mental health. His policy included domiciliary visiting before admission, early discharge, and frequent out-patient and domiciliary follow-up. In the Severalls area, by contrast, there was virtually no community contact of this kind. Netherne's reputation was based chiefly on its services for longer-stay residents.

Administrative indices, such as length of stay and number of community contacts during the five years, demonstrated the expected differences between Mapperley and the other two hospitals. Against the hypothesis, however, a shorter stay and a higher contact rate after discharge were not associated with a better outcome at follow-up. In part, this seemed to be because the extra community contacts in Nottingham were not focused principally on the most disabled or needy people and families.

The principles worked out through trial and error by the pioneers of the '50s and '60s, consolidated by the results of research into methods of rehabilitation and family care, led to a vision of 'best practice' in community psychiatry. It should be based on, first, 'state-of-the-art' knowledge of the causes (biological and psychological impairments and social disadvantages) of social disablement associated with the manifestations of mental illness or handicap; second, on knowledge of the ways in which such causative or sustaining factors can be prevented, reduced or contained; third, on an understanding of how staff and services can most effectively identify people with mental health problems, assess their needs for various forms of treatment, enabling and care, and meet these through the provision of services that do not themselves impose further disability.

The third of these principles itself has three parts. A community service should be geographically responsible, so that it can be based on an epidemiological understanding of local needs. It should be comprehensive, with a range of facilities and skilled staff wide enough and flexible enough to cope with the variety of need. It should be integrated, with an organisation and administration capable of ensuring adequate continuity of care with economy and efficiency.

These principles also provide a structure for evaluating the results of care (Wing, 1990*b*).

The concept of ladders or stairways is useful in formulating both the functions and the possible structures of services. Residential, occupational and recreational needs can be visualised in terms of three stairways, each with landings at different functional levels, with rooms leading off for recuperation and rehabilitation. At the bottom of all three are facilities for severely disabled people with the highest dependency needs. Those who reach the top have no need of any specialist services. The stairways have aids to help disabled people to mount at an appropriate pace or (if all the steps are in place) to prevent a precipitate fall to the bottom at times of relapse. These aids – assessment, treatment, enabling, care, welfare supplements, social support – are provided by professional and informal carers.

At the peak of their reputation, the best hospitals provided most of these steps and the aids to go with them. A variety of residential accommodation was available in addition to wards, and occupation was seen as the key to rehabilitation. At Netherne, for example, a register was kept to ensure that every resident had the opportunity for occupation during working hours and for recreation at other times. Regular assessment enabled each patient to make what progress through the system was individually possible. If no further movement could be achieved, the level of functioning that had already been achieved was recognised as requiring active maintenance. At the most basic level, there was housing, heat, light, food, clothing, privacy, the use of extensive grounds, and a reasonable degree of protection for people vulnerable to exploitation and cruelty.

These were the innovative processes that could be fully applied only if the 'shell' within which they operated was extended and fundamentally changed. The stairways did climb out of the hospitals to hostels, day centres and out-patient and domiciliary care, but the top end of the system was largely devoted to the rehabilitation of people who had become 'long stay' in former times. Once these had been resettled, the placement of those who were 'difficult to place' became the problem.

In the new era of 'early discharge', which was well under way in Nottingham in the mid-1950s, follow-up studies demonstrated that early discharge from the security of a good hospital would only be generally successful if the stairway system could be recreated, step by step, with all the landings, bannisters, chairlifts and network of formal and informal carers in place – but 'in the community'. Since part of the 'old' long-stay population need not have stayed so long if, in former times, there had been alternatives to the hospitals, it seemed probable that somewhat smaller numbers would accumulate in a new system. Moreover, by no means all hospitals were as advanced as the best, and a policy of run-down to closure as new community services were put into place might well be the most economical way forward.

It should be emphasised that this vision did not depend on a romantic view of the community as *Gemeinschaft*. It was based on an expert and experienced grasp of the nature of the disabilities that afflicted people with severe (and particularly with chronic) mental disorders. A further point for emphasis is that there has been no major advance in the theory or practice of psychosocial methods of treatment, enabling, care or support during the past 30 years. There has been refinement, consolidation and systematisation, but the principles remain those first worked out in the mental hospitals themselves and in the early studies of patients discharged from them.

Reality

Monitoring progress

The Social Services Committee of the House of Commons submitted its second report on community care in 1985. Members visited services all over England and Northern Ireland and ended a rather critical review with a list of 101 recommendations. The remark "any fool can close a hospital" is perhaps the most pointed and best-remembered phrase in the report. Members did not mean that it is managerially easy to close a hospital with a minimum of disruption and human suffering, but that the positive task of building the alternatives is far more difficult than the negative one of closure. Nevertheless, the negative goal seemed to them often to have been paramount. Recommendations 92–99 dealt specifically with the need for research and for the establishment of a proper information and monitoring system. The latter point was reinforced by Sir Roy Griffiths (1988), who asked for a government monitoring office.

One way to measure progress is to set targets. In its 1975 white paper on mental health ("Better Services for the Mentally Ill') the government was thoughtless enough to do so, laying down 'norms' (which later, more cautiously, became 'guidelines', and then disappeared altogether) for appropriate numbers of places in a variety of service settings per 100 000 of the national population. The indices were crude, and it could be suggested that those for alternative residential care were too low, but they had the merit of being available for public discussion and criticism. The Audit Commission (1986) accepted the opportunity by arguing that, between 1974 and 1986, insufficient progress had been made towards the targets for homes and hostels (70.1% of target number of places filled), day centres (31.9%), and day hospitals (39.9%).

Robertson (1981), who prepared a memorandum of guidance for statisticians working for regional health authorities, calculated (assuming no radical changes in service practice) that, by the end of 1991, an average health district would generate 140 in-patients per 100 000 inhabitants, 80 of whom would have been resident for more than one year, including some 'from the old days'. If those with dementia were omitted, there would be 53 short-stay and 53 long-stay patients per 100 000. Of the latter group, 32 would be under and 21 over the age of 65. If, for 'in-patients', we read 'people with high dependency needs', we have an approximate, probably minimum, guideline for the numbers needing quite costly alternative services.

These are national figures, but it is evident that there is much local variation. A working party of the Royal College of Psychiatrists (Hirsch, 1988) found a high correlation between admission rates to psychiatric hospitals and an index of deprivation based on the census statistics of the health districts they served (Jarman, 1983, 1984). The index is an amalgam of the three major sociodemographic indicators – poverty, social isolation and ethnicity.

Cumulative psychiatric case registers, which collect high-quality information about the contacts made with services within a defined geographical area, should therefore be excellent instruments for local planning. A recent compilation of data and research from eight such registers provides detailed evidence concerning local variations (Wing, 1989). Of particular relevance are the bed-occupancy figures for the group of hospital residents that has become known as the 'new' long stay. Although the name sounds static, the process of new accumulation is dynamic. The rate of 'recruitment' to long-stay status (a stay of one year in hospital) is particularly crucial for those interested in hospital run-down.

The English and Welsh register areas can be grouped according to their population growth or decline during the 60 years between the censuses of 1921 and 1981. At one end of the spectrum comes Oxford, a highly attractive area that has doubled its population during that time. It is closely followed by Worcester. At the middle of the range come Cardiff, Nottingham and Southampton – medium-sized industrial cities close to the national sociodemographic average. Then come Salford, part of the Greater Manchester conurbation, and finally Camberwell in inner London, where the population has halved in 60 years and the area covered is part of the sixth most deprived health district in England. There is a high correlation (0.76) between rate of recruitment to new-long-stay status and the eight-item Jarman index of deprivation.

More recently, research into the run-down to closure of Friern and Claybury Hospitals has shown a very similar spread of rates of recruitment across the health districts served and an almost identical correlation with the Jarman index (Graham Thornicroft, personal communication).

National 'norms' cannot, therefore, be used for district planning without detailed consideration of local sociodemographic characteristics, population trends, and service traditions. In addition, hospital statistics become less and less useful indicators of need as run-down continues. The few psychiatric case registers now remaining are precious assets because they collect high-quality information from all or most of the specialist facilities serving their areas, including those managed by social services and charities.

The impact of run-down and closures on care for people who are at risk of long-term disability but who have never been long stay in hospital is now as important as (perhaps more important than) the immediate impact on those who have to be moved out in order to close the hospital.

Research has become more difficult. Sampling frames and measures of need have to become more sophisticated (Brewin *et al*, 1987; Wing, 1990*b*). Intensive research into the effects of run-down and closure, together with the build up of alternative services, has been rather scanty.

The closure of Darenth Park Hospital

The best documented study so far is a ten-year assessment of the progress made by 890 adults with a mental handicap, resident in Darenth Park Hospital in August 1980 (Korman & Glennerster, 1990; L. Wing, 1990). By then, run-down from the peak of over 2000 residents was already well advanced. Using the results of earlier research by the Medical Research Council (MRC), it was possible to match very closely the salient needs of residents who left during the first five years with those of others who remained behind. Most placements during this time were made *ad hoc*, into existing forms of residential care. After 1985, purpose-built accommodation was made available.

As in other studies, people with the fewest problems were resettled first. Those with more difficult behaviour who left early were mostly transferred to a disused smaller hospital. The interim follow-up results were rather different, according to type of setting. A few private hostels were said to be of a very low standard, appearing to be run for profit above all else. Others were run by highly motivated individuals, dedicated to the care of mentally handicapped people, but a question arose as to continuity when the owners retired. The group homes ranked high on personal independence but had poor ratings for educational activities and occupation compared with the hospitals and NHS and social-services hostels. Relatives tended to be reasonably satisfied with the current placement, whether in hospital or elsewhere.

Much depended on the actual location of accommodation. For example, people in units with large grounds had more freedom of movement than those in a small house in a busy street, where the front door had to be kept locked for safety reasons. Small houses also had disadvantages if people with challenging behaviour were mixed with others, as was sometimes the policy. Neighbours were by no means always friendly and staff turnover was high. Korman & Glennerster (1990) concluded that costs were higher in the community.

On the whole, there were no dramatic changes in the handicaps, behaviour or skills of residents, in either those who left or those who stayed. There was a strong impression that the major factor determining outcome was the pattern of disabilities present initially. The hospital regime was not rigid or restrictive and there were good opportunities for occupation, recreation and exercise. Most benefit from resettlement was experienced by those least handicapped, who enjoyed their greater freedom and were able to use some of the local amenities.

Data from the final follow-up of the original cohort, including the second phase of resettlement, are now being analysed. This will provide a clearer picture of the effects of purposeful community placements for people with the most serious problems. Above all, however, it is already obvious that the needs of individuals differ greatly. Planning must be based on a close understanding of different types of handicap and skill.

Powick Hospital

The only other detailed example of independent research into community services intended to replace the functions of a hospital that has actually closed is that of Powick. The planning background is described in Chapter 8. It is sufficient to note that the recommendations made in 1970 following a feasibility study were based on the ideas and the practice briefly outlined in the first section of this chapter. The proposals were gradually implemented with the aid of substantial central funding and the services now in place are more comprehensive than in most districts in the country.

Apart from the work of the Worcester Psychiatric Case Register (Chapter 12) a small MRC team has studied facilities for long-term (more than a year) day attenders under the age of 65. This group, like the one that accumulates in long-stay residential alternatives to hospital wards (Ryan, 1979; Wooff, 1990), provides an important index for the success of care in the community. Long-term day care in the Worcester and Kidderminster districts shows some interesting features. First, it is relatively plentiful compared with other health districts, and is mostly provided in day centres (136 out of the sample of 184), not day hospitals as in the rest of the country (Edwards & Carter, 1979). In the survey, the commonest diagnosis was schizophrenia (59 out of 184), followed by neurosis (45). The third most frequent group included 35 attenders with mainly neurological disabilities, who had the highest average problem count of all diagnostic groups and were nearly all in day centres, although facilities for their care were not optimal. On average, attenders spent only 12 hours a week at the day units. The milieu provided was warm and supportive but the useful social-club function might more often have been linked to targeted rehabilitation efforts. The relationship between number of problems (as judged by care staff) and hours of attendance, though positive, was not as close as might have been expected, and a similar generalisation could be made about the number of unmet needs. Relatives and attenders tended to describe more problems than did staff, who were not necessarily well informed about life outside the centre.

These results have a general relevance for day-care policy locally and nationally and will be described in detail elsewhere. A second study, of the opinions of general practitioners concerning the changes in the Worcester Development area, has now been published (Bennett, 1989). Most general practitioners had no special interest in psychiatric work but attitudes towards the subject were generally favourable. Most of those who remembered the former service thought there had been an improvement. The main criticisms were that it was difficult to obtain emergency admission to hospital, social workers were slow to respond to calls for help, and community psychiatric nurses did not provide sufficient information about their work with people on the family doctors' lists. That there are still gaps in provision is shown by the recording during the research of a significant number of mentally ill people who were destitute and by the presence of many others in hostels for 'homeless single people' (George Milner, personal communication). This problem has been most thoroughly documented in inner-city areas (Leach & Wing, 1980) but it has recently been described even in Oxford (Marshall, 1989).

In summary, this is the most promising example to date of the feasibility of carrying through a closure policy intended to improve services (Wing *et al*, 1988). Whether the injection of substantial central funds, and the fact that the area is relatively privileged, allows this conclusion to be generalised to more deprived parts of the country remains to be seen. Julian Leff (Chapter 4) presents data on research into the run-down to closure of Friern and Claybury Hospitals. This work is particularly important because of Friern's situation in a deprived area of north London.

How far down the road?

Seen from a 30-year perspective, one must conclude that progress towards community care, defined in terms of services that are both independent of large hospitals and better than the best available when the ideas were being formulated, has been promising but not spectacular. Some of the most important obstacles to progress have not been reviewed here. They include: failure to understand the nature and scope of the social disablement associated with mental disorder; denigration of the functions of asylum; inappropriately divergent philosophies of social and medical care; central guidance to managers that emphasised closure as the aim (negative targeting) rather than providing a workbook showing how to set up the alternative first; low priority within both health and social services, compared with other pressing priorities; too short a timetable once closure had been decided; lack of provision for evaluation and learning from the results; shortage of funds to undertake such a gigantic task.

The Worcester Development Project, culminating in one of the first closures and the establishment of a service that for all its gaps undoubtedly works, is a reminder of what can be achieved given a collaboration between strong local motivation and central-government interest and funding. With the passage of new legislation on the National Health Service and the transfer of responsibility for community care to local authorities, it remains to be seen whether more, or less, priority will now be given to ensuring that processes that were new 30 years ago will be fully implemented within an appropriate 'shell'.

References

AUDIT COMMISSION (1986) *Making a Reality of Community Care*. The Audit Commission for Local Authorities in England and Wales. London: HMSO.

BENNETT, C. (1989) General practitioner satisfaction with a new community service. *Journal of the Royal College of General Practitioners*, **39**, 106–109.

BREWIN, C., WING, J. K., MANGEN, S. P., *et al* (1987) Principles and practice of measuring needs in the long-term mentally ill. *Psychological Medicine*, **17**, 971–981.

BROWN, G. W., BONE, M., DALISON, B., *et al* (1966) *Schizophrenia and Social Care*. London: Oxford University Press.

EDWARDS, C. & CARTER, J. (1979) Day services and the mentally ill. In *Community Care for the Mentally Disabled* (eds J. K. Wing & M. R. Olsen), pp. 36–59. Oxford: Oxford University Press.

GRIFFITHS, R. (1988) *Community Care, Agenda for Action*. A report to the Secretary of State for Social Services. London: HMSO.

HIRSCH, S. (1988) *Psychiatric Beds and Resources. Factors Influencing Bed Use and Service Planning.* London: Gaskell.

JARMAN, B. (1983) Identification of underprivileged areas. *British Medical Journal*, **286**, 1705–1709.

—— (1984) Underprivileged areas. Validation and distribution of scores. *British Medical Journal*, **289**, 1587–1592.

KORMAN, N. & GLENNERSTER, H. (1990) *Hospital Closure. A Political and Economic Study.* Milton Keynes: Philadelphia.

LEACH, J. & WING, J. K. (1980) *Helping Destitute Men.* London: Tavistock.

MARSHALL, M. (1989) Collected and neglected. Are Oxford hostels for the homeless filling up with disabled psychiatric patients? *British Medical Journal*, **299**, 706–709.

POWELL, E. (1961) Address to the National Association for Mental Health. In *Emerging Patterns for the Mental Health Services and the Public.* London: NAMH.

ROBERTSON, G. (1981) The provision of inpatient facilities for the mentally ill. A paper to assist NHS planners. Unpublished. London: DHSS.

RYAN, P. (1979) Residential care for the mentally disabled. In *Community Care for the Mentally Disabled* (eds J. K. Wing & M. R. Olsen), pp. 60–89. Oxford: Oxford University Press.

SOCIAL SERVICES COMMITTEE OF THE HOUSE OF COMMONS (1985) *Community Care with Special Reference to Adult Mentally Ill and Mentally Handicapped.* Second report of the Committee. London: HMSO.

WING, J. K. (ed.) (1989) *Health Services Planning and Research. Contributions from Psychiatric Case Registers.* London: Gaskell.

—— (1990*a*) The functions of asylum. *British Journal of Psychiatry*, **157**, 822–827.

—— (1990*b*) Meeting the needs of people with psychiatric disorders. *Social Psychiatry and Psychiatric Epidemiology*, **25**, 2–8.

—— & BROWN, G. W. (1970) *Institutionalism and Schizophrenia.* London: Cambridge University Press.

——, BENNETT, C. & CUMELLA, S. (1988) *Worcester Development Project.* Report to DHSS on Research. MRC Social Psychiatry Unit (unpublished).

WING, L. (1990) *Hospital Closure and the Resettlement of Residents.* Aldershot: Gower.

WOOFF, K. (ed.) (1990) *Residential Needs for Severely Disabled Psychiatric Patients. The Case for Hospital Hostels.* Mental Health Information Unit, Salford Health Authority.

3 Government policies

JOHN REED

Mental health and mental illness services continue to be a priority for the National Health Service (NHS), and occupy a very high political profile. There were four debates in the House of Lords in the early part of 1989 on mental health issues, and ministers take a very close personal interest in the problems of the mental health service.

Government policies for mental health were first stated in 1961 by the then Minister of Health, Enoch Powell, in what became known as his 'Watertower' speech. In 1968, the Minister at that time, Kenneth Robinson, said that progress in modernising the organisation of mental illness services was lagging behind progress in applying modern methods of treatment. He proposed the Worcester Development Project to demonstrate how the problems of transition from the old to a modern mental illness service could be identified and solved in a co-operative exercise between local health authorities and local government.

A feasibility study was produced in April 1970 and, from this, the Worcester Development Project was born. It is exciting now to see the project's fulfilment and how, despite the inevitable difficulties, co-operation between health authorities, local authorities, voluntary agencies, carers, and sufferers has led to a really successful development.

Government policy was stated more fully in the 1975 White Paper "Better Services for the Mentally Ill" and with minor amendments, this remains the statement of present policy. In 1981 the government paper "Care in Action" identified three main tasks for health authorities in developing services for the mentally ill. These were: (a) to create a local, comprehensive mental illness service in each district, reducing the catchment area of multi-district mental illness hospitals to their own district; (b) to create a psychogeriatric service in each health district; and (c) to arrange for the closure of those mental illness hospitals that are not well placed to provide a service for their local district and that are already near the end of their useful life.

It is by no means a matter of chance that the development of local services is mentioned before the closure of hospitals, which is not a primary aim of present mental health policy. However, the resident population of mental illness hospitals has fallen dramatically over the years, from just over 152 000 in 1954, to just over 60 000 in 1986. This fall started long before the publication of present policies, and indeed signs of the change were to be found before the arrival of the major tranquillisers. As the population of mental illness hospitals has fallen, because of better treatment and through the death of those elderly patients who spent a long time in hospitals, so it may be sensible to close some hospitals to ensure the best use of resources. Ministers are adamant, however, that no hospital should close until better services have been provided to replace those that it gave, and here the Worcester Development Project is an example of how this can be done.

Britain spends a great deal of money on mental illness. Health authorities spend some £1.1 billion per year, while 25% of the total drugs bill of the Family Practitioners Service is for psychiatric and related disorders. Local authorities spend more through hostels, day-care schemes and social services. Social-security payments for those with psychiatric disorders are very substantial and increasing. Mental health care is a huge enterprise.

Having established the policy, we have to be sure that it is working across the country as we would want it to; those at the centre need a clear picture of what is going on locally. As part of the initiative announced in July 1989, the Department of Health has been working collaboratively with regional health authorities to identify the progress that has been made in implementing mental health policy and the problems that have been encountered. The purpose of this is not to recriminate over any past inadequacies, but to identify what the Department needs to do to help health authorities implement policy effectively. On the basis of this work, ministers will consider whether there are any further steps that it is right and practical to take to improve the care of mentally ill people.

The situation is not static. Present policy has been of major benefit to the great majority of mentally ill people and is the right and humane policy, but we must take note of and respond to areas of current anxiety and concern. Firstly, there is the problem of long-term mental illness. The government, in responding to the Social Services Select Committee Report on Community Care in 1985, agreed that the real measure of the success of a service was not whether it met the needs of those who *least* need its activities, but whether it met the needs of those who *most* need them. One group of people most needing the service are those who suffer long-term and serious disability because of mental illness. The advent of neuroleptic drugs and other improvements in treatment has meant that many people who would previously have spent months or years in hospital now become well enough to be discharged quickly. Although new treatments have led to great improvements in clinical outcome, the evidence for an improvement in the rate of *cure* for common and serious illness, such as schizophrenia, is slight. It remains likely that following a first attack of schizophrenia, the majority of sufferers will be left with a degree of disability that may at times be severe, and many are likely to need continuing care. In ensuring that such patients, when discharged from hospital into the community, receive the continuing care that they require – with as much certainty and with the regular reassessments of their needs that would have been available to them had they remained in hospital – is a major challenge to all services, whether these are based in district general hospitals (DGHs) or mental illness hospitals.

It is clear from many accounts, both in the scientific press and in the media, that this does not always occur. Reports show that up to 50% of destitute homeless people are suffering from serious mental disorder (Timms & Fry, 1989) and that an untoward number of mentally ill people are in the prison system (Coid, 1984). Often, these problems are attributed to a shortage of beds for mentally ill people as the consequence of hospital run-down and closures. However, at the end of 1986, there were, in England, some 10 000 empty, staffed psychiatric beds and some 8000 vacant places in day hospitals. Faced with statistics such as these, it is hard to avoid the conclusion that part of the problem is one of effective distribution of resources, rather than an overall shortage of beds or places. Moreover, in the accounts of destitute, homeless mentally ill people and those in prison, although some may report having been discharged to a hostel for the homeless, a much commoner story is that they have been discharged from hospital to suitable accommodation and care, and later lost touch with the services. It is a failure of continuity of community care that appears to be a common feature behind many such cases.

Recognising the difficulties in ensuring continuity of care in the community, the Department of Health has, over recent years, commissioned research into this problem in Salford, Southampton, and Hackney. Ministers have received reports of these and other projects and, with the intention of improving continuity of care in the community, the current NHS planning guidelines require each health authority, as a new service objective, to establish 'care programmes' by 1991 for those chronically disabled by mental illness and living mainly in the community. As a policy aim, each health authority is also required to identify a consultant with special responsibility for continuing care and rehabilitation. Further guidance on this subject will deal with the topics of case management, community review, and the use of computerised registers of those at risk.

Asylum, in the sense of a safe refuge, is a necessary part of any comprehensive service, but this refuge can be provided in many settings besides an institutional one: not all those who need asylum need the same type of refuge. A range of options is needed to provide asylum, both in the community, through different types of supported accommodation, as well as through long-term in-patient care. It is widely believed that present policy sees no role for such in-patient care for younger mentally ill people, but this is not so. Since 1975, there has been mention of hospital hostels in policy documents and over the years, the Department of Health has funded research into the ways in which this long-term in-patient care can be offered to highly dependent patients, in ways that avoid some of the problems of conventional long-stay wards.

Some mentally disordered people need treatment in conditions of such high levels of security that this can only be met in the Special Hospitals, established specifically for that purpose under the NHS Act. There are at present some 1725 beds in the four Special Hospitals, and these are managed directly by the Department of Health. The appropriateness of this arrangement has, in recent years, been subject to increasing debate and to critical scrutiny within government departments, the health-care professions, by academics, and by groups representing the interests of patients in particular and the public in general. After review of the management arrangements for the Special Hospitals, a special health authority has been made responsible for the management of a national special-hospital service and general management has been introduced within the hospitals.

At a more clinical level, published research at Broadmoor Hospital (Dell & Robertson, 1988) has suggested that care in a Special Hospital is no longer appropriate for many of the patients there. Further research, coupled with an assessment of the mental health needs of the prison population and of what is available within the NHS, both in the regional secure units and elsewhere, will provide a sound basis for determining the need for treatment facilities which offer varying degrees of security. These will range from Special Hospitals at one extreme, to intensive-care units or beds in DGH units and mental illness hospitals at the other. Two regional health authorities are developing plans for a network of intensive-care psychiatric facilities in all their district services.

Only a small proportion of people with significant psychiatric disorder are referred to the secondary-care services: of 230 people attending their general practitioner with significant psychological symptoms, only 17 will be referred to psychiatrists and only six admitted to hospital (Goldberg & Huxley, 1980). Clearly, it is important to ensure that the general practitioner and primary-care team are well equipped to detect and treat psychiatric disorder. There is good evidence (Johnstone & Goldberg, 1976) that better detection and treatment of affective disorder by the primary-care team leads to improved outcome and lessened burden on patients and on their families.

The dilution and diversion of secondary-care skills to deal with more minor psychiatric morbidity in primary care is a cause of anxiety. Of course, both ends of the spectrum of illness do need to be dealt with: they need early detection, accurate assessment, and effective treatment. But we need to establish cost-effective ways of detecting and treating minor psychiatric morbidity by primary-care teams so that the secondary-care teams, including community psychiatric nurses, continue to focus mainly on the severely mentally ill. Furthermore, secondary-care teams should develop an important role in educating and supporting primary-care teams in their increasing involvement in the care of mental illness, both major and minor, and in preventive initiatives. For both mentally ill and mentally handicapped people, community care is as essential an element of a comprehensive range of local services as is hospital care. Both need to be provided in balanced proportions. Overprovision of in-patient facilities cannot compensate for underprovision of community care, any more than community care is likely to operate effectively without supporting hospital services.

In the development of our knowledge of the nature of a modern psychiatric service and of the successes and problems of such a service, both the Worcester Development Project itself and the evaluation of the service by the professorial department in Birmingham and by the MRC Social Psychiatric Unit have been very influential.

References

COID, J. (1984) How many psychiatric patients in prison? *British Journal of Psychiatry*, **145**, 78–86.

DELL, S. & ROBERTSON, G. (1988) *Sentenced to Hospital: Offenders in Broadmoor*. Oxford: Oxford University Press.

GOLDBERG, D. & HUXLEY, P. (1980) *Mental Illness in the Community: The Pathway to Psychiatric Care*. London: Tavistock.

JOHNSTONE, A. & GOLDBERG, D. (1976) Psychiatric screening and general practice. *Lancet*, i, 605–608.

TIMMS, P. & FRY, A. H. (1989) Homelessness and mental illness. *Health Trends*, **21**, 70–71.

4 Evaluation of the closure of mental hospitals

JULIAN P. LEFF

The lessons that can be learned from creating community services in Worcester cannot be assumed to apply to an inner-city district. That is why it is necessary to evaluate services not just in one place, but in a variety of places with different social and economic conditions.

This chapter concerns the closure of two mental hospitals. In 1983, the North East Thames Regional Health Authority (NETRHA) decided it should close two of its six mental hospitals. The total number of in-patients in each hospital had declined from over 2000 to around 800 – about a third of their peak capacity. The Authority had to decide which hospitals to close, and it did so on interesting grounds. Each hospital was given ratings on a number of factors, one of which was the cost per head of patients: the higher the cost per patient, the more likely the hospital would be chosen for closure. The argument is, of course, that one must get rid of hospitals that are expensive, but the hospitals that were most expensive were the ones that had improved their conditions most. Another factor that influenced their choice was the backlog of repairs. Finally, they chose two hospitals, Friern and Claybury, out of the six. The Regional Medical Officer announced this decision in July 1983, on television. The consequence was that many of the staff were very alarmed and in Claybury, the consultants refused to co-operate with the closure plans for six months.

Friern was built in 1851, opened by Prince Albert, and designed for a thousand patients. By 1950, it had more than double the number it was built for; as a result, it was overcrowded, as happened to many of these mental hospitals. It was in fact these slum conditions that became the target of many of the sociologists' objections to large institutions: they were looking at hospitals that were not functioning in the way they had been designed to do. But since the 1950s, with the onslaught of public and sociological opinions and scandals, bed numbers began to decline. In Claybury Hospital, the decline began in 1951 or 1952, before the introduction of chlorpromazine. There is no doubt that the neuroleptic drugs aided this decline, though they did not initiate it. The decline averaged 50 beds per year until 1983, when the decision was made publicly to close the two hospitals. The decline then levelled off for a few years, but then resumed. The scandals that have developed in America about community psychiatry, and the new discipline which is called 'street psychiatry' – going out to the homeless psychotic patients living on the streets of major cities, with sandwiches and pills with the hope that the patients will swallow both of them – are well known. That situation though, is not due to excessively rapid emptying of the hospitals: the rates in the US and the UK are exactly the same. It is to do largely with the lack of cheap rented accommodation, which has been disappearing from the major cities.

The question facing us was how can you close hospitals that are serving very deprived inner-city areas? We were able to persuade the Regional Health Authority to put money into evaluating its own policy. We made the point that any large business or industry puts 1 % at least of its income into research and development, and any government organisation or national organisation ought to be doing that as well. However, to cover the period of closure would mean at least 10–11 years of research, and in 1989, the team's costs were about £150 000 a year. So over the course of ten years, it will cost about £1 ½ million; on the other hand, it is answering some vital questions that no one else has confronted so comprehensively.

The research team consists of psychiatrists, psychologists, a psychiatric nurse, sociologists, and health economists; it is looking at three different aspects of the closure. One is the straightforward question – is it good or bad for the patients? The second is – how expensive is hospital compared with community care? If the two are put together, the result is a cost/ effectiveness analysis. The third question is a socio-political one. What is the most effective way of organising and developing the new services? This involves a sociological study of the decision-making processes, which in itself is an innovative venture.

To answer the clinical question – is it good or bad for the patients? – it is necessary to inquire who is left in the mental hospital, after many years of declining bed numbers. Considering first the 'old long-stay' patients, since the number in hospital had declined by two-thirds, there must be twice as many in the community who have been discharged over the last 40 years as there are currently in hospital. When a census of Friern Hospital was conducted in 1983, it was discovered that about 40% of the 'old long-stay' had already had a spell living in community provision. In other words, they were failures of the current methods of community care.

The accumulation patients, or 'new long-stay', are a residue of 'short-stay' patients, both from the psychiatric hospital itself, and from the local district general hospitals. If psychiatric hospitals are to be closed, where are these patients then to be accommodated? One can only guess what proportion they are of the short-stay group: perhaps one-twentieth, but it might be one-hundredth. It depends very much on the catchment area. In a salubrious place like Worcestershire, there may be very few 'new long-stay' patients, but in an inner-city area, like Camden or Islington in London, there are many people who have no home to go to, and a high proportion of these are mentally ill.

The first thing one has to do is to ask questions about the patients remaining in hospital: "What are their disabilities?", "What are their assets?", and, not to be forgotten, "What do they think of their care, and where they want to live?" If that is not done, it will merely perpetuate the paternalistic attitudes of the old institutions.

Closing a mental hospital and replacing it with community facilities is a vast natural experiment, which is going on nationally and internationally. However, it is an experiment that has not yet been evaluated comprehensively (Thornicroft & Bebbington, 1989). We do not have as much control over our research as we would like to have: we cannot randomise patients to discharge and non-discharge groups, at least not on a large scale. It may be possible in some facilities to do that, but our research team could not for two reasons. One was regional policy. The policy makers laid down two guidelines for creating community services. One was they must be in small-scale, domestic-style facilities. The second was that patients must move with their friends, but that is not as easy to determine as one might think. How can it be decided who is a patient's friend?

So it was necessary to make do with another kind of research design – a matching of 'movers' and 'stayers': a patient who is due to be discharged is matched as closely as possible with someone who is still in the hospital and likely to stay there for at least a year. What measures should be selected on which to match the two groups? This is a difficult question, because they should be closely matched on those variables that will predict success in the community. However, it cannot be known what those variables are until the study is finished in ten years. So we have to make educated guesses: age, sex, length of stay in hospital, total length of admission to hospital, and severity of social disability were in fact chosen.

Patients were followed up for at least a year, and the measures then repeated. This design assumes that people who stay in hospital are in a stable environment, but that, of course, is incorrect, since the hospital environment is not stable. Firstly, once the decision is made to close a hospital, it suffers from 'planning blight'; nobody wants to spend money on it, and the hospital's physical environment rapidly deteriorates. Staff start to leave. Anybody with their eye on the future does not want to stay in a hospital like that, and anybody in a senior position who is close to retirement wants to take it prematurely. So staff morale goes down.

On the positive side, the staff know that every patient has to leave, if death does not occur first. Therefore, they begin to make more focused efforts to rehabilitate the remaining patients; patients who may have been neglected for years become the focus of attention.

So there are two opposing influences – deterioration of the physical and staff environment, but an attempt to improve the patients' functioning.

One set of changes is being compared against another set of changes, not against a static population. We need to know what has been made available in the new service, and to be able to compare it with the hospital facilities. We need to know how' well or badly the patients do in the community, in terms of social and clinical measures, and to examine the quality of the caring environment. In particular, there is a focus on those aspects of the caring environment that have been called 'restrictive practices' in institutions.

For this purpose, some well established schedules were adopted, but others had to be developed *ab initio*. The schedules include one on personal information and psychiatric history, which collects data on the demographic and clinical characteristics of the patients in the past. However, assessing the mental state is a problem, since a high proportion of long-stay patients are dominated by negative symptoms, and there is no completely adequate instrument for measuring these. The one chosen was the Present State Examination (PSE), which, although not dealing very adequately with negative symptoms, is well established internationally. About one-third of the patients at Friern and a quarter at Claybury could not be interviewed at all. When the research worker sat down and tried to talk to them, they either got up and walked away, were mute, or talked incomprehensibly. This gives rise to quite a serious lacuna in the data.

The population being studied is an ageing one, with all the physical illnesses that the ageing have. The researchers were very concerned that when these patients go into the community, they may not get as close a scrutiny of their physical health as in a psychiatric hospital, where nursing staff are present all the time to observe them, and junior psychiatrists act as general practitioners (Brugha *et al*, 1989).

As there was a need to assess social behaviour, the Social Behaviour Schedule (SBS) was used, but it was found to have gaps; these concerned behaviour that was discouraged or for which there was no opportunity in the hospital, including budgeting with money, shopping, and cooking. So a new schedule had to be created – the Basic Everyday Living Skills Schedule, which attempts to assess the patient's ability to do those things for which, in hospital, they often have no opportunity.

The Environmental Index was derived from a number of previous attempts to measure restrictive practices in institutions. Are there set times for going to bed? Are the doors locked? Do people have personal possessions? In addition, questions are asked about the environment outside the hospital. A psychiatric hospital provides for the leisure of the patients, and is surrounded by grounds for them to walk in, which are very valuable amenities. In the community, how easy is it for patients to get to a park? Do they have to cross a main road? Do they have to take a bus to get to the day centre?

With regard to patients' attitudes, doubt has been cast on the ability of psychotic patients to answer for themselves. In a pilot study, the Patient

Attitude Questionnaire was given to 40 subjects, and we went back six months later and readministered it. To our surprise, it was found that two-thirds of the questions were answered in exactly the same way, and in only 15% of the questions were the answers delusional or apparently arbitrary. So one can rely very firmly on patients' ability to speak for themselves and to convey what they want.

However, some doubt remains about how valid it is to ask someone, ''Do you want to leave hospital and live in the community?'' if they have been in the hospital for 30 or 40 years. How do they know what is on offer in the community? They are making a hypothetical choice, and that probably gives rise to an underestimate of the number who would like to live outside if they knew enough about it.

Finally, there is the Social Network Schedule. A way had to be found of defining who was a patient's friend. There are some social network scales already in existence, but they are for neurotic patients, and the social life of a psychotic patient differs totally from that of neurotics. Consequently, a new schedule had to be devised, and this has turned out to be one of the most crucial instruments in the whole investigation. First, a time budget is constructed: the patient is asked to recall what he/she did the day before and at the weekend, and this generates a set of social contexts. Within each social context, we ask who they have seen within the past month. This provides a list of names, defining the social ambit of their life. With respect to each person, we then ask, ''Would you miss that person if you never saw them again? Would you visit them? Is your interaction with them just saying 'hallo', 'goodbye'? Do you do things for each other? Do you actually have full conversations? Do you consider them to be a friend? And are they someone you can confide in, someone you can tell your innermost thoughts and worries to?''

This batch of schedules was used to collect baseline data on all the long-stay, non-demented patients in the two hospitals, amounting to 770 (NETRHA, 1988); this procedure took two years. Analysis of duration of stay showed that one-third had been in hospital between one and five years, but there were roughly 10% in each subsequent ten-year duration band. There was no obvious fall-off over time, as might have been expected. Consequently, there were still about 10% of the patients who had been between 40 and 50 years in hospital. Five had been in more than 60 years, and one patient, who was over a hundred years old, had been in hospital for more than 80 years!

The sex ratio showed a predominance of males in both hospitals: the modal age was between 60 and 65, and the age distributions were very similar. In the two hospitals, just over 50% have been in-patients for more than 20 years. A high proportion of the survey population are single, and only 3–4% are married. Originally, about 40% came in involuntarily, both males and females, but currently a very low proportion, approximately 6%, are detained under the Mental Health Act.

In considering diagnoses, it must be emphasised that these are the products of dozens of different psychiatrists, who have different diagnostic habits. It is therefore remarkable to note how similar the two hospitals are in this respect. Eighty-one per cent in both hospitals had a diagnosis of schizophrenia, and 6% one of affective illness. Neurosis and personality disorder accounted for 4% in both hospitals and organic brain disease 2–3%. The PSE data exhibit the same kind of concordance. In 3% in both hospitals, no psychiatric diagnosis was possible, while 3–5% had mania, 36–37% clear-cut schizophrenia, and a large group (26–29%) possible schizophrenia. These latter are patients in whom a psychosis is suspected, but there is insufficient evidence to diagnose it; the reason is that they are largely patients with negative symptoms, or who are concealing their active psychosis. The PSE subscores present much the same picture – those with active delusions and hallucinations constitute about a third in the two hospitals.

Does mental illness subside with duration of stay? Does 'burn-out' exist in this population? In fact, no convincing picture was found of a clear decline in psychotic features over time. Overall, exactly a third in both hospitals had active delusions and a quarter had active hallucinations. This indicates a high proportion of patients with florid psychosis, rather than being burnt-out cases, which presents a serious problem for community placement.

In respect of the social disabilities or social behaviour of these patients, it is remarkable that of the 20 items on the SBS, there are only two on which the two hospitals differ significantly. In Friern, a higher proportion of patients show severe problems with concentration, and in Claybury a higher proportion express odd ideas. From the point of view of public concern, which focuses on odd or peculiar sexual behaviour and violence, those are at the bottom of the list, with 5% or less showing these problems.

The two most common serious problems are poor hygiene, shown by over half the patients in both hospitals, and socially inappropriate forms of behaviour. The relative prevalence of social problems in the two hospitals is astonishingly similar, with the rank order correlation being 0.93.

In terms of physical problems, a high proportion of patients (25% in Friern and 12% at Claybury) suffer from incontinence, and it must be stressed that these are not demented patients. Why the problems should be worse at Friern is uncertain; it might reflect a greater use of neuroleptic drugs.

Analysis of patients' attitudes revealed that a third want to stay in hospital, a third want to leave, and a third cannot make up their minds. These findings raise the problem of what to do with patients who say they do not want to leave the hospital. It is possible that a clear presentation of what is available in the community might change the minds of some.

Finally, there are the data from the Social Network Schedule. A pilot study with this instrument was conducted on a community sample of 30 patients who were being seen by community psychiatric nurses. These 30 patients spoke to a total of 415 people, at least monthly: of those, they said that 339 would be missed, 235 would be visited, 131 were regarded as friends, and 97 as confidants. This suggests a hierarchy of social significance. Data from the two hospitals showed that the size of the patients' social networks varied enormously – from 1 to 34 in Friern and to 61 in Claybury. However, the median network size was very similar – eight and nine in the two hospitals respectively. About 20% said they have no friends whatsoever, and two-thirds or more mentioned no hospital staff in their networks: in other words, they do not even speak to hospital staff once a month. Three-quarters have no relatives in their network, and 90% or more no contacts in the community. These findings depict a very socially deprived group of people, and furthermore, the data exclude more than a quarter of the patients from whom no answers could be obtained to the schedule. It is reasonable to assume that these non-responders are the most socially deprived of all.

These findings indicate that the process of discharging long-stay patients, over 30 or 40 years, has left behind a very similar group of people in both hospitals. Therefore, the problems faced by those who want to create a new service in the various health districts are very similar. This is an additional benefit for the research, because it enables comparison of what has been provided across different districts.

During the first two years of this evaluation, 161 long-stay patients were discharged from the two hospitals: 90% of these were successfully followed up, with interviews of patients, or carers, or both (NETRHA, 1990). Only three patients have not been traced, and these are assumed to have become vagrants; in fact, all three led a vagrant life before their current admission. The death rate among the discharged patients was no higher than among their matched 'stayers'. No patient committed suicide and none had been to prison. There were no significant changes in the movers, compared with the stayers, in psychiatric symptoms, physical health, social disabilities, or social networks. However, the movers were living in significantly less restrictive environments than the hospital wards, and this was reflected in a much higher proportion who wanted to remain in their community accommodation.

These benefits in terms of quality of life and client satisfaction were not costly to achieve. The economic analysis showed that community provision for these patients was marginally cheaper than hospital care for the first two years after discharge.

An increasing proportion of the discharged patients are being accommodated in ordinary houses, bought by the health authority or a housing association and converted for the use of 3–12 patients. Staff are on duty in them during the day, and sometimes also at night, if necessary. This is likely to be the predominant form of accommodation for the next few years of hospital run-down.

The last issue to be considered is what might be called the 'skimming-off' process. It is human nature to discharge the easiest patients first. In the first year of the project, about a third of the Friern patients who were discharged were 'new long-stay', while in the second year, almost half of the patients were. This means that the patients who had come to hospital fairly recently were being moved out in preference to those who had been in hospital for 20 or 30 years. This process has continued in the third year, with the result that the patients who have been discharged are considerably better on a number of characteristics than those remaining. A major consequence of skimming-off, however, is that it cannot be assumed that the relative success of reprovision in the first two years will continue throughout the period of closure. In particular, we are concerned that the most sociable patients, the ones with the largest social networks, have been discharged first, leaving behind an increasing proportion of asocial individuals. It is uncertain at present whether it will be possible to form viable groups in the community from such isolated people.

References

BRUGHA, T. S., WING, J. K. & SMITH, B. L. (1989) Physical health of long-term mentally ill in the community. Is there unmet need? *British Journal of Psychiatry*, **155**, 777–781.

NORTH EAST THAMES REGIONAL HEALTH AUTHORITY (1988) TAPS evaluation of reprovision for Friern and Claybury Hospitals. *Progress Report to the Mental Health Services Evaluation Committee, 1985–88.* London: NETRHA.

——— (1990) One-year follow-up of discharged long-stay patients. *Report of TPAS 4th Annual Conference, 1989.* London: NETRHA.

THORNICROFT, G. & BEBBINGTON, P. (1989) Deinstitutionalisation – from hospital closure to service development. *British Journal of Psychiatry*, **155**, 739–753.

5 Management of district psychiatric services without a mental hospital

C. PHILIP SEAGER

This chapter gives a broad overview of a typical psychiatric service, comments on the organisation of districts – in particular 'independent' districts – and discusses the management of such a service.

What is meant by a 'typical' psychiatric service? In the first place, it should be comprehensive. Secondly, it needs to be based in the community, but there are complicated issues about the various processes of development in this direction, with different degrees of progress in different places. Regional and district health authorities have produced ten-year strategic plans, with the names of mental hospitals expected to close by 1991–94: this applies to about two-thirds of the hospitals that have been in existence for over the past 100 or so years. The Department of Health's proposal is that those in the centres of their populations, which are accessible, and which are linked with a district general hospital (DGH) should be retained. This applies to about one-third of the total, but some districts have ignored these guidelines and still propose to move towards basing their services in DGH units.

The DGH units were probably in their heyday in the 1960s, especially in the (then) Manchester Hospital Region, which was very keen to promote the idea of such units. That regional board also supported the great transition in Lancaster Moor Hospital, which changed it into a general hospital, not by removing the psychiatric patients, but rather by importing general hospital services so that orthopaedic and ophthalmic services were actually in the mental hospital. That was one of the early attempts to modify the pattern of standard large mental hospitals (Smith, 1961).

One of the problems about linking psychiatric services with general hospitals was that the psychiatric unit was often built into the fabric of the hospital with, for example, a medical ward below, a gynaecology ward above, and an ophthalmic ward at the side, but not the facilities that are required in a comprehensive psychiatric unit. This was also true of some day hospitals, which were not situated in the community but instead were linked with the general hospital. They were often described as having 90 places (or, as the Dutch call it, 90 chairs), but those '90 places' usually meant that there were 70 for the in-patient unit and only 20 for actual day patients; it was an artificially inflated figure.

With the move to more specific community services, the new terms 'community mental health centres' and 'community resource centres' have been introduced, but it is not always clear what is meant by these terms and which services are actually provided in them. Sometimes, there is a 'mini-hospital' with beds, day places, and rehabilitation and treatment activities, whereas others constitute a management centre for all kinds of activities in the community, sometimes acting as a base for the staff without providing any treatment facilities. Another important element is the 'non-health-service' component – links with social services, housing, voluntary agencies, probation, education, the police, and of course the man in the street.

This typical service might be represented geographically, situated in a mythical 'Southern Regional Health Authority', adjoining the boundary of the neighbouring 'Eastern Regional Health Authority'. One can picture the former 'Bromfield Area Health Authority', with its large mental hospital, having been split up into districts, so that there is 'North Bromfield Health Authority', 'East Bromfield Health Authority', 'Treadgate Health Authority', together with 'Blimpington Health Authority', which happens to be over the border in the 'Eastern Region' but has traditionally made use of the Bromfield mental hospital. Links have to be made with the various areas, perhaps South Loamshire and West Blimpington of the 'Loamshire County Council' Social Services Department. The boundary difficulties which are implied by this geographical arrangement are by no means uncommon. Because it wishes to become independent of the mental hospital, 'East Bromfield Health Authority' suddenly has to provide its own psychiatric services. The mental hospital itself is running down, reducing its long-stay wards, and requesting health authorities and social services departments to make provision for their former residents, who may have been in hospital for decades. Self-sufficient services have to be developed locally, with their effects on provision of social services, primary health care, and the specialist medical services of the DGH.

Services for the mentally ill, particularly the elderly mentally ill, and also those for elderly people with physical illness, do not always fit easily into the likely management structure of a district. This is particularly true if the structure is based on institutions. One then finds that different portions of the service are managed by different unit general managers, and it can be difficult to provide a cohesive pattern of care for all those in need. In a large district, an appropriate pattern may be to have a mental illness management unit, but should this include the elderly mentally ill, or are they more appropriately linked with the unit managing services for the elderly? The same question may be asked concerning child psychiatry. A community unit may also be seen as an appropriate lodging for mental illness services, but this may split day hospitals and community psychiatric nursing from the DGH psychiatric unit.

It can be seen that there is no 'right' answer to these management issues. In larger districts, a unit for psychiatric services is probably most appropriate, or possibly one for priority care services, including those for the elderly. Any decision must ensure that adequate communication is maintained between the various components of a comprehensive psychiatric service, both in hospital and in the community. It is particularly important to avoid isolation of the community psychiatric nursing team from the main body of psychiatric services, and to ensure links with the primary-care team, including district nurses and health visitors.

With the planned closure of large mental hospitals, attention must be paid to a strategic programme of replacement of their services. Buildings form one component, but the process of change affects all categories of staff, who must inevitably be anxious about their jobs, their future, and proposed different styles of working. Complex financial arrangements are inevitable when there is such a major change in methods of treatment and care. Financial provision may be derived from the sale of the hospital, once its services are unnecessary. This money can be available for the mental health services of the various districts, bearing in mind the Department of Health's ruling that ensures that money raised from the sale of 'mental illness' land is to be devoted to psychiatric services in other parts of the district. The system of bridging loans from region and the 'dowry' system, which passes money from hospital to community to provide support for discharged patients, is now well established, although failure to meet target dates and redirection of resources may occur.

Those districts whose psychiatric services were originally dependent on a central mental hospital may run into particular difficulties in terms of the required range of staffing and of appropriate advice. The extramural service may have been provided simply by one or two out-patient clinics, which had little need for nursing or paramedical support, but staff for these services are now necessary. Yet recruitment may be difficult, in the absence of firm plans for the future, and any staff available may have limited experience of the current issues of psychiatric care, while newly appointed staff may, in their early days, also have limited experience.

Managers may find difficulty in getting appropriate clinical opinions about the direction in which patient care should be moving. This is particularly true in the non-hierarchical organisation of consultant psychiatric practice. Each doctor may have strongly held views, but it is important that, through a division of psychiatry or similar medical committee, an agreed pattern of development should be reached, to avoid management acting independently of clinical advice because this is not clearly defined and coherent. Management must be aware of the reasons for difficulties in getting a single psychiatric voice, but psychiatrists must recognise that advice will be sought elsewhere if continued vacillation and contradictory views militate against a clearly defined medical policy.

Another aspect of the management of change is represented by the fact that people directly involved in the process are often late in knowing and appreciating the changes that are to occur. An explanation may be the need to avoid 'planning blight', which can cause considerable distress and discomfort for individuals who have to suffer during the period when decisions are being made. A shared philosophy is necessary for the services that are being modified, and in this respect, health authority staff frequently have a different ethos from social services staff. The former have the view that patients need looking after, to a greater or lesser extent – a paternalistic view; the latter have a philosophy of choice – people must be asked what they wish to do, and this may be carried to lengths which result in demented individuals being expected to have an opinion and to take responsibility for the decision which is made. Inevitably, a balance must be found between these two extremes, and the skills of professionals in this field lie in making the right judgement about the degree of dependence or independence of any individual at a particular time. While this same judgement has to be made concerning the sharing of information about hospital closures and transfers, it is equally necessary to have the correct balance between sharing all discussions and avoiding alarm, when various possibilities are being looked at without any firm decision being contemplated.

All services, particularly those involving people who are suffering from some degree of psychiatric incapacity, should be monitored to ensure that there is public awareness of the way in which treatment and care are provided, within the context of the many demands for resources. Such monitoring is included in the activities of regional and district health authorities, as well as of local authorities. In spite of this, the experience of the Health Advisory Service suggests that if it is actually being carried out, it is not very effective, because there are pockets of patient care and social-services provision which fall far below an acceptable level. Whatever changes take place in the future, it is important to have some form of external appraisal, whereby a group of independent professionals reviews the services for a district and comments on their acceptability for the tasks in hand, as well as offering advice on improvement, where appropriate.

By their very nature, district services have the advantage of being local (although in some very large districts, this localisation may not be apparent), but this brings in its train a different type of problem. Provision of services for relatively small groups of individuals may be uneconomic and may be difficult to provide. Examples are mother-and-baby units, services for substance abusers, those for behaviourally disturbed individuals, and for mentally handicapped people with psychiatric problems. A judgement has to be made about whether it is more appropriate for a group of districts to provide a single, central service with shared professional input, or whether the general psychiatric services can offer sufficient specialised knowledge to ensure that these individuals receive the best possible treatment.

Educational and research facilities may also come into this category. The stimulation and enthusiasm engendered by young, enthusiastic, inquiring students of all professions may be lost if a centralised academic institute is seen as the most appropriate solution to the production of future generations of professional staff.

A most important issue in the development of psychiatric services is the relationship between hospital and community services. As psychiatry becomes more community orientated, the dispersal of trained staff may result in a loss of professional skills. Many primary-care teams are pleased to have the services of community psychiatric nurses, clinical psychologists, occupational therapists, and social workers, all of whom make an important contribution to treating the psychological morbidity that forms a major part of the work of the primary-care teams. The work of Goldberg & Huxley (1980) indicates that out of every 1000 people in the community, in one year, 250 experience some form of 'dis-ease', and 230 of them go to the general practitioner or a similar form of health care; 140 of these have a psychiatric or psychological disorder detected, but only 17 are referred for a psychiatric opinion, of whom six are admitted to hospital.

If the psychiatric services are moving into the field of primary health care, a definition of roles must be of great importance. Either the primary-care services are going to be relieved of the major proportion of their work, while the secondary psychiatric service is going to be swamped, or else the professions formerly working in the psychiatric services will move into primary health care to relieve some of the burden of psychological ill-health, leaving the secondary services devoid of experienced staff. It is apparent that there is no shortage of demand for services; the decision that has to be made concerns the best use of the available expertise offered by all the professions working in the field of disorders of mental health.

Consideration must also be given to services for patients under general medical and surgical care who are suffering from various types of psychological or psychiatric disorder. In the past, psychiatrists had little contact with the general hospital because they spent much of their time in the mental hospital. However, with the development of DGH psychiatric units, there were more opportunities for psychiatrists to make contact with their other medical colleagues, and in many places an active liaison service has developed. If psychiatry again moves from the general hospital, this time into community mental health services, this contact with general medicine may be diminished, resulting in less awareness of the potential services on offer for people who may benefit from them.

Apart from any proposals arising from the white paper "Caring for People", which is directed at community care in the next decade and beyond, there is no doubt that services for the mentally ill are in a great state of flux. This makes enormous demands on the professional staff, who have to adjust to different models of working, modify their attitudes and relationships with professional colleagues, and be available to offer sound, practicable judgements to management about the appropriate directions of change.

References

GOLDBERG, D. & HUXLEY, P. (1980) *Mental Illness in the Community: The Pathway to Psychiatric Care.* London: Tavistock.

SMITH, S. (1961) Psychiatry in general hospitals. *Lancet, i,* 1158–1159.

6 Change from institutional to community care in Torbay

JOHN JENKINS

Exminster Hospital was built in 1845 as the Devon County Lunatic Asylum, serving about three-quarters of a million people. In 1845, it took two days to get there from Barnstaple, some 50 miles away. In the hospital, some people lived for many years in single rooms opening off a corridor; in 1977, the beds in some wards were actually touching each other.

In 1982, it cost £7 million a year to run Exminster Hospital; there were 800 staff and 600 residents. Exeter Health Authority Mental Health Services cost just under £12 million in all, so that 58% of the budget was spent on maintaining the hospital. Of that, just under half was spent on hotel services. This model of care was no longer meeting the requirements of the mentally ill.

The money was going into the wrong place. Much of it was not being spent on patient care, but – for instance – on pumping steam endlessly around miles of corridors. The health authority decided that it would reallocate the resources according to the requirements of the populations of the three areas served (North Devon, Exeter, and Torbay), and calculated that £2 million should be spent in North Devon, £5.5 million in Exeter, and £4.5 million in Torbay. Between 1982 and 1987, money was directed from the institution into community services in these three areas. The flow of cash was arranged on a quarterly controlled basis. A financial model showed what money was available in considerable detail – divided into that spent on direct patient care, and that spent on overheads and on the central departments running the hospital. Thus, all £7 million formerly spent on Exminster Hospital was channelled into providing community services in Torbay and North Devon, while the money formerly spent on Digby and Wonford Hospitals – the other psychiatric hospitals in the health district – was channelled into providing Exeter services.

In 1981, the Authority devised a staffing policy for the mental health service. The main elements were: (a) there was to be no compulsory redundancy; (b) a personnel package was agreed to assist staff in taking part in the new service, including practical arrangements such as removal expenses for moving home and families (for many miles in some cases); (c) training packages were devised to help staff become more aware of the principles of community care and to reorientate them as necessary. In Exminster Hospital, 731 staff were in post on 1 April 1984, whereas two years later, 491 were in post, the majority working in the new community services.

Most staff did not believe that closure of Exminster was going to happen, having 'heard it all before' over the last 20 years. However, communication channels were changed from existing committee meetings to monthly open meetings continuing over five years; every member of staff could come to them. These discussed plans, progress, people's anxieties, and the problems that they could foresee for themselves, the patients, or the organisation. Attendance ranged from 200–300 in the early days to no more than 10 in the later stages. Individual interviews were held with each member of staff at least four times, to encourage them and reassure them about their future. In 1984, the new jobs were advertised within Exminster Hospital; everybody knew where they were going to be, in some cases two or three years in advance. Only 25 people decided to take early retirement, and only ten refused to co-operate with the changes.

Torbay was divided into five localities and within each, it was planned to provide a comprehensive local service, easily accessible, and responding to all the needs of people there with mental health problems. In each mental health centre, a multidisciplinary team was established, and the centre is the access point to which local people are referred or to which they refer themselves.

The capital developments which replaced the beds at Exminster are scattered throughout the county of Devon. Sometimes, ordinary public buildings such as leisure centres, community centres, or church halls have been used to provide the location for day care. For example, in Newton Abbott, we had a hostel for the mentally ill, a standard unit for the elderly with 20 beds and 10 day places, and a unit on a small industrial estate to provide work experience in boat building and printing. In Torquay, the mental health centre is in the middle of the town, and the unit for the elderly in the grounds of the district general hospital.

There was a small core of people who had been in the locked ward in Exminster for 10–30 years, and it was felt that they could not be put in hostels in residential areas. These damaged people, who had not responded over many years to various forms of treatment, were placed in a unit (Watcombe Hall), run on behaviour-therapy lines and with 11 acres of grounds. Four of those six people are still there, but two have moved to more independent living; the remaining four have shown some response to the new milieu, albeit slowly. There are also acute in-patient beds in the grounds of the district general hospital. Services for people with drug and alcohol problems are provided in Torquay.

Exminster closed in 1987.

II. Powick Hospital, St Wulstan's Hospital, and the Worcester Development Project

7 The history of Powick Hospital

PETER HALL

In 1830, John Connolly, who was Professor of Medicine at the University of London, recommended that all persons on insane lists should be visited at home by an asylum medical officer at least once in 15 days and at least once in seven days in recent cases. Also, he said, "if it was represented that a keeper was required, a keeper should immediately be sent from the establishment". It would be very difficult to think of a clearer description of the sort of services that psychiatrists are trying to provide today, not only in Worcester, but in Madison, Sydney, and elsewhere.

The wheel seems to have turned full circle from community care in the 17th century, through private asylums in the 18th, public asylums in the 19th, and community care again in the 20th century. There are about 1000 beds in private nursing homes and rest homes in Worcester Health District, which the health authority inspects just like 18th-century predecessors. The legislation is almost identical. I have no doubt that in the 21st century, there will be another public asylum of some sort in Worcester.

The first local madhouse was, in fact, private. It was built in Droitwich in 1791 in what is now Ricketts Lane, but at that time was known as Asylum Lane, and it is now a working-men's club. Charles Hastings, the famous Worcestershire physician who founded the British Medical Association, is less well known for having been President of the Medico-Psychological Association, the predecessor of the Royal College of Psychiatrists. He was also co-proprietor of the Droitwich Asylum with William Ricketts, a surgeon. Their asylum housed 104 patients; it was quite large in size and its first-class apartments, including a servant and "every proper indulgence suitable to the patient's disorder", cost four guineas a week, a considerable sum in those days (Parry Jones, 1972).

By 1849, the Commissioners in Lunacy were expressing great dissatisfaction with the Droitwich Asylum, which had initially been a place of some repute. Many of its patients were therefore transferred to Powick, when that asylum opened. An advertisement which appeared in the *Medical Directory* for 1852 under the names of Sir Charles Hastings and Martin Ricketts, stated that "in consequence of the removal of the pauper lunatics from this establishment to the new county asylum, appropriate arrangements will be made for receiving an additional number of second and third class patients". Third-class patients paid one guinea a week and were not allowed tea! In neighbouring Hereford, by contrast, a lunatic asylum had already been erected by public subscription in 1787. It was established under the same administration as the Hereford Infirmary, so that it was among the first psychiatric units within a district general hospital group.

The Municipal Acts of 1774 and 1808 had allowed county magistrates to inspect private madhouses and later to build asylums at the expense of the county rates. This became mandatory under the Lunacy Act 1845. At the Worcester Michaelmas Sessions of 13 October 1845 (on the motion of John Somerset Beckington, the then Member of Parliament) the Worcester magistrates set up a committee to consider erecting an asylum for pauper lunatics. They looked into the prospects of joining Warwick or Hereford, but concluded that "the inconvenience of such a union would be so serious as to make it most desirable that they should be avoided". The truth was that Hereford had already agreed to join Monmouth, while Warwick was not prepared to consider the proposition. The committee resolved that a third of lunatics should be permitted to remain in workhouses, because they were harmless, and that "admission should at all times be given to new and curable cases". They decided that a new building should be constructed in "an open and airy situation within 5 miles of Worcester Shire Hall, and that it should be accessible by good roads". They succeeded in finding a magnificent location, with an idyllic view of the Malvern Hills to the southeast. It also had the required supply of good water, and was achieved by the purchase for £2800 of an estate in Powick, owned by a Mr Stallard, and called White Chimneys. The Commissioners of Lunacy's rules stated that there must be grounds of at least one acre for every ten patients, and that "the wards of mental hospitals must be so arranged that the Medical Officer might pass through all of them without retracing his steps" (Harvey, 1987).

The purpose of the asylum was "not only to alleviate the suffering of unfortunate individuals who may require protection and care, but also the means of effecting cure in large proportion, thereby restoring them to their families and friends".

The original plan had airing courts for the violent and dirty, a second airing court for the imbecile and epileptic, and – near the medical superintendent's office – a third one for the tranquil and the convalescent! The elevations of the new asylum drawn by the architects, Messrs Hamilton and Medland of Gloucester, were of a very attractive building, in the Georgian style.

As in the case of the Egyptian pharoahs, the subsequent history of the hospital is best understood by considering the reigns of each of its medical superintendents. According to a writer of the time, a medical superintendent "must be a man of dominist will who can compel obedience by the sheer force of his own strong nature" (Bynum *et al*, 1988). The first medical superintendent was engaged at a salary of £350 plus coal, candles, laundry, and vegetables. There were about 60 candidates, but no interview. The appointments committee just looked at the papers, which was perhaps a shame, because Dr I. R. Grahamsley, the first medical superintendent, who came with very good references, possibly had some personal problems. He had been trained at the Royal Morningside Asylum in Edinburgh by Thomas Clouston, and presented the governing committee with a detailed list of recommendations, written in beautiful copperplate, after they had sent him to study the asylums in Lincoln, Shropshire, Bedford, Surrey, Leicester, and Oxford. Although the story is still shrouded in mystery, it is certain that he committed suicide in July 1854 by swallowing prussic acid. It seems that this may have been because he had been criticised for having appointed his sister-in-law as matron of the hospital, at the princely salary of £40 per annum. His obituary appeared in the *British Medical Journal*, 25 September 1854. After him was a locum, a Dr Tooklake of the Norfolk Asylum.

The asylum had opened on 11 August 1852, although in fact it was not completed until October 1853. The patients themselves made many of the bricks and laid out the beautifully terraced grounds; during 1852, 175 patients had been admitted, most of them transferred from Droitwich. In April 1853, the Lunacy Commissioners reported, with satisfaction, that there was not a single patient under restraint. The Commissioners also pointed out that only one patient was in seclusion, that the patients were remarkably free from "maniacal excitement", and, perhaps most important of all, that there had been a great improvement in the quality of the beer. Private patients were charged 15 shillings weekly.

Dr James Sherlock, the second medical superintendent, was appointed in September 1854, having previously been in charge of James Moray's private asylum in Perth, and he improved even on Dr Grahamsley's enlightened regime. In his day fishtanks, birdcages, flowering shrubs, and games were placed in the airing courts. However, the hospital's water supply was not as abundant as had been hoped. This was because the then central planners had insisted that the local builders, who actually knew the place, dig a very deep well, which proved not to contain much water. On 29 November 1854, the hospital had its first serious cholera epidemic.

The nursing attendants were all artisans, such as tailors, shoemakers, bakers, butchers, and carpenters. Male and female staff were not allowed to mix, and were fined one penny for every three minutes they were late for work. They would often work 20 hours out of 24, for a wage of about £20 a year. As they had to sleep on the wards, they were also on call at night. Male patients had to be shaved twice a week (Hassall & Warburton, 1965).

The library, which had previously contained "a large store of books, almost exclusively religious in nature, was supplemented with more secular books and even weekly publications". Parties of patients and staff were taken on excursions. In 1862, "on the occasion of the wedding of the head male attendant, a ball was held in the laundry, where upwards of 150 patients were regaled with plum cake and gin punch and dancing took place from 7 o'clock until 11.30 pm''. About two-thirds of the patients were engaged in some kind of work – domestic, building, or on the hospital's farm, at that time extending over 552 acres. The growth of public confidence was such that patients who had been concealed by their families were brought to the hospital: ironically, this led to the build-up of a nucleus of chronic patients and crowding. As a result, the hospital had to be enlarged, and became more institutional. The extensions were very different from the original Georgian building, being cheaply built, with unplastered walls and huge wards, which were still causing problems over 100 years later. Some roofs were thatched.

In 1879, Sir Edward Elgar became bandmaster to the hospital, at a salary of £36 per annum. He had been a member of the staff band from 1877, when he was 20 years old, as had been his father and uncle. He would arrive once a week – on horseback – on Saturdays, hold rehearsals, stay overnight, and conduct the band at a concert on Sunday afternoon, to which the county would be invited. He was paid 2 s 6 d for writing a polka or a waltz, of which he composed a good many ('The Powick pieces'). In later life, he apparently observed that ''the experience of writing for a haphazard and often unpredictable combination of instruments was a valuable discipline for an aspiring composer.''

Dr Sherlock died in 1881 of gout, said to be ''generated by 30 years of conscientious discharge of laborious and trying duties''. He was only 53 and according to his obituary in the *British Medical Journal* (28 May 1881) had been an able physician, with a ''peculiarly suave, courtly and attractive manner''. His funeral was attended by most of the doctors in Worcester and Malvern, and movingly, their wreath stated that he had been ''loved by them as a brother''.

He was succeeded by Dr Marriott Cooke (later Sir Marriott Cooke, KBE), a graduate of King's College, who had been medical superintendent of the Wiltshire Asylum in Devizes. He had not particularly wanted to be a psychiatrist, but an obstetrician, and only came to Worcester to get some psychiatric experience. However, he stayed for a very long time and in 1898 became a national Commissioner of Lunacy. His committee were so impressed that they gave him a certificate to the effect that they wished thus to testify that in their opinion, they possessed a superintendent ''second to none in the kingdom'', and doubled his salary (Obituary, *British Medical Journal*, 31 October 1931, p. 829). He died in 1931, in his 80th year. He had a staff of three doctors, which was exceptionally large for the period, one of whom was Hubert Bond, later Sir Hubert Bond, one of the architects of the Mental Treatment Act 1930 and later involved in a celebrated law suit (reported in *The Times*, 1 March 1924, *Bond & Adam* v. *Harnett*).

Sir Marriott Cooke was succeeded in 1898 by Dr George Braine-Hartnell, a Middlesex graduate, who had been his senior assistant medical officer. In his day, Powick became so big and crowded that it was decided to erect another asylum in the northern part of the county, to take the overflow. It was named Barnsley Hall Hospital, rather than Barnsley Hall Asylum, because it was decided to make provision for private patients. Of the 167 patients admitted there in July 1907, when it opened, 149 were again transfers, this time from Powick. It is ironic that the original Worcester Development Project Feasibility Study suggested that all the residual patients from Powick should be dumped in Barnsley Hall Hospital again.

Towards the turn of the 20th century, things had become generally less rosy. There was an increase in involuntary committals and like most asylums (Foucault, 1965), Powick became a handy place in which to put the awkward, the unwanted, the useless, and the potentially troublesome. In cold weather the temperature could not be raised above 60°F (16°C) in the wards. In particular, there was still a scarcity of water, which had to be carted in. There was a severe typhoid outbreak in 1889. Even by 1921, only boiled water could be drunk. Idle and disorderly persons could be committed to the asylum for being "unable to give a good account of themselves", a phrase that was still evident in the notes when I arrived in 1963.

The old records – written in copperplate and calf-bound – give some idea of clinical matters at the turn of the century. One of them refers to Samuel H, a miner, who was admitted on 22 August 1896. His son had been an in-patient, his sister was also an in-patient, and at the time of his admission there was a three-week history of his wandering about and stating that "God had mixed him in a bucket by mixing three glories". He was examined on admission by a Dr Bubb (the third assistant medical officer), who found a systolic murmur at the aortic area. This seems quite accurate, because poor Samuel died at 7.40 p.m. on 30 December 1909, of left heart failure, this having been treated with ether and ammonium chlorate.

The 1890 Lunacy Act was nearly perfect from the legal point of view, but it reflected the increasing loss of faith in the asylum, as well as its fearful image in the public imagination. Early treatment, easier methods of admission and frequent discharge were no more. The 'moral treatment', gentle rewards, treatment with vegetable emanations, and firm discipline which had marked the mid-19th century disappeared (Walton, 1979), despite the hopes originally expressed about them, which were very similar to our own hopes of 'care in the community'.

In 1920, Dr Braine-Hartnell was succeeded by Dr Felix Fenton, another Edinburgh graduate and a prominent local Freemason and ex ship surgeon, who had been appointed assistant medical officer in 1907. He died on 21 April 1958, having spent 43 years at Powick. In his day, the utmost economy was exercised: Powick became the cheapest mental hospital in the country and prudent councils from all over the country sent their patients there. This was still an enormous problem half a century and more later, as such patients were almost impossible to discharge to community care. The asylum became increasingly overcrowded, the atmosphere more and more repressive, and even the medical superintendent's quarters, Bredon House, was used as an auxiliary hospital, housing 34 medically discharged soldiers. Whilst, no doubt, patriotism was a motive in this, mental patients from the forces were paid for at an extra 2 s 6 d a week. Out-county patients at that time were costed at 14 s 6 d a week, while the actual cost was only 9 s 5½ d, which was a handsome profit. The hospital was also selling a thousand bushels of wheat and 18 000 lb of beef per annum at that time (Matthews, 1984).

This expansionism was not merely confined to numbers; institutionalisation had taken on an impetus of its own. Chronic drunkenness and other vices, which had previously been regarded as sins, became increasingly 'medicalised'. The asylum had stopped being a hospital, and had become a kingdom over which the medical superintendent held sway, managing it with justice and economy, using administrative, or in modern terms, managerial rather than clinical skills (Bynum *et al*, 1988). "All manner of decrepit, socially inept, and incompetent people were increasingly admitted, and the suggestion that incorrigible petty offenders and chronic drunkards were sick was understandably attractive to despairing prison governors and penologists" (Scull, 1981). Nothing ever changes in this dialogue of penologists and psychiatrists, nor in what is now termed 'income generation by hospitals'.

By 1930, there were still only four doctors at Powick. The hospital was still lit by gas and the nursing staff still lived and slept on the wards. Dr Fenton apparently had strict moral views, and it is said that he would patrol the hospital shrubberies on Sunday evenings armed with an umbrella, to make sure that the nurses were not getting up to mischief. He had been strongly influenced by a Dr Graves, who was then medical superintendent of Rubery Hill Hospital, Birmingham, and a great believer in focal sepsis. Dr Graves would visit Powick frequently, and most patients consequently had their tonsils, gall-bladders, and most of their teeth extracted on admission.

At their visit on 26 February 1941, the Commissioners of the Board of Control were critical. They mentioned the "large proportion of difficult patients with destructive habits", the lack of occupational therapy, and the fact that only six male patients and no female patient had parole. The Commissioners also complained about the low admission rate, the cold and the lack of armchairs, although they did add that Dr Fenton had "given much thought to air raid precautions", and that "the diet was full and varied". It had consisted of roast beef, potatoes, swedes, rice pudding, and jam on the day of the Commissioners' visit, but I have it from more than one member of staff at the time that much of the time the food consisted of milk and bread, and that it was considered that otherwise the patients would become too strong and difficult to manage. The only occupational therapy other than farming or domestic work was a knitting class, which was said to be held in enforced total silence; the matron was only allowed four pairs of stockings each month for nearly 600 female in-patients.

In 1950, a new medical superintendent was appointed, Dr Arthur Spencer, who had previously been deputy medical superintendent of St David's

Hospital, Carmarthen. He had first qualified in pharmacy at Bath, and was a Baptist lay preacher, who had been attracted, as a then intending missionary, to medicine. He then qualified at Bristol and won the Gold Medal for Surgery. In the 1950s, he and Dr Ron Sandison, his deputy, developed treatment with LSD, after Dr Sandison had visited Switzerland. According to the *Worcester Evening News* of 18 May 1954, LSD "enables a patient to recover his early childish memories. He is thus able to get out of his system the unhappy memories which are often the cause of nervous disturbances in later life." The report states that "LSD was astounding. The most soul-searing experience I have ever had". During its 'LSD phase', the hospital became known internationally, and even certain famous film stars arrived for treatment at its LSD Department. Dr Sandison also started the Samaritan Movement in Worcester. Dr Spencer and he unlocked the hospital completely, despite opposition from the medical and nursing staff, and founded a social work department. Dr Spencer discontinued the practice of the nursing staff living and sleeping on the wards (Obituary, *British Medical Journal*, 23 June 1979, p. 1718).

Interestingly, the 1844 address, 'White Chimneys', was still entered on death certificates, to avoid stigma. There was a good deal of suspicion of Dr Spencer's views. He had been a socialist county councillor in Camarthen and it was rumoured that he had been a communist. The *Sunday Mercury* of 9 June 1966 quoted him – very characteristically for those of us who knew him – as stating that "the contraceptive pill must be free for all young, unmarried people so that unwanted children are not born". In his and Sandison's time, Powick Hospital not only gained worldwide recognition, and perhaps a degree of notoriety, for its research with LSD, but also pioneered the treatment of schizophrenia with thioridazine. The nursing school was also revived in 1950, having been one of the earliest such schools in the 19th century and having issued diplomas well before the national one by the Royal Medico-Psychological Association.

In 1963, the untimely death in his early 40s of Dr John Jeffreys, a senior hospital medical officer, opened the door for my own appointment, of Dr Dennis Currie, and that of Dr Max Harper, as the hospital's first National Health Service consultants. I was jointly appointed by the health authority and the University of Birmingham, leading to the strong links between the hospital and the University, which are still evident. Amongst other things, I soon started our first day hospital, St Anne's Orchard (which is still a day hospital) and became involved in the use of the then new depot antipsychotic drugs. By 1964, the number of in-patients had reduced to 890, compared with 1100 in 1954. This progress was accelerated by the arrival of Dr George Milner in 1966 and Dr Huw Richards in 1968, as further consultant appointments.

In May 1968, there was a television programme in Granada Television's series "World in Action", which drew attention to (but grossly exaggerated) the poverty of the amenities in some of Powick's wards, which great efforts had so far failed to remedy, after so many years of excessive economy.

More happily, the hospital's active and progressive clinical service was also noted. The then Minister of Health decided that Powick would be the 'test-bed' for a new type of service, but before finally leaving this story, it is perhaps important to point out that the development of the service would have continued, even without the Worcester Development Project. By 1972, when Dr Spencer retired, most of the new service was in place, and Powick Hospital stopped admitting patients on 5 December 1978. As in the case of several of his predecessors, Arthur Spencer just survived to see the next phase of progress. He died on 11 May 1979. It is interesting, and perhaps ironic, that at the closure of Powick on 7 March 1989, the 20 patients remaining were rehoused in a luxurious, small residential unit in Droitwich, not a mile from the place where, on 11 August 1852, 175 patients had moved from Hastings' & Ricketts' madhouse to Powick.

Acknowledgements

I am indebted to numerous friends and colleagues for their support, advice and help. Prominent amongst them were Anthony Wherry, Tom Pope, George Marshall, Ron Sandison, Patricia Allderidge, Mrs P. A. Bonnett and Wendy Schwab. Worcester City Archives provided some of the material for this chapter.

References

BYNUM, W. F., PORTER, R. & SHEPHERD, S. (1988) *The Anatomy of Madness*, vol. 3. London: Routledge.
FOUCAULT, M. (1965) *Madness and Civilization*. London: Tavistock.
HARVEY, N. (1987) The Lunacy Commission, 1845–60. Unpublished PhD thesis, University of Bristol.
HASSALL, C. & WARBURTON, W. A. J. (1965) The new look in mental health – 1852. *Medical Care*, **2**, 1–4.
MATTHEWS, G. (1984) The public response to poverty, vagrancy and lunacy in Worcestershire 1870–1920. Unpublished PhD thesis, University of Birmingham.
PARRY-JONES, W. L. L. (1972) *The Trade in Lunacy – A Study of Private Madhouses in England in the 18th and 19th Century*. London: Routledge and Kegan Paul.
SCULL, A. (1981) *Madhouses, Mad Doctors and Mad Men – The Social History of Psychiatry in the Victorian Era*. London: Athlone.
WALTON, J. K. (1979) Lunacy in the Industrial Revolution. *Journal of Social History*, **13**, 1–22.

Further reading

CRAMMER, J. (1990) *Asylum History. The Buckinghamshire County Pauper Lunatic Asylum – St John's*. London: Gaskell.
HUNTER, R. & MACALPINE, I. (1963) *Three Hundred Years of Psychiatry 1535–1860*. London: Oxford University Press.
LADER, M. & ALLDERIDGE, P. (undated) *The History of British Psychiatry 1700 to the Present*. Welwyn Garden City: Smith, Kleine and French.

8 Closure of the Worcestershire asylums and their replacement by a new community-based service

PETER HALL, DEENESH KHOOSAL, RAYMOND GILLARD, ROGER POWELL, DAVID BATTIN and HUW RICHARDS

The closure of the asylums

The Worcester Health District has had to close *two* large mental hospitals, both situated in the Malvern Hills – St Wulstan's and Powick. The closure of the former had a very important effect on that of the latter, rather like the mysterious effects of some unseen celestial object on planetary orbits.

St Wulstan's Hospital was originally built for the treatment of American psychiatric casualties in World War II, and it then functioned as a tuberculosis sanitorium until 1961. It was in fact also the evacuation centre for the Queen Elizabeth Hospital in Birmingham in case of nuclear warfare. There were plans to make it a geriatric hospital, but it actually became the West Midlands Regional Psychiatric Rehabilitation Centre, under the distinguished directorship of Dr Roger Morgan. The aim of this hospital was to foster social and vocational readaptation, and in its day it attracted many visitors from both home and abroad. It originally had 230 patients, but over the course of time, there seems to have been a gradual reduction in the number of outlets to which patients could be discharged, and the large mental hospitals of the West Midlands, a little belatedly in some cases, began to develop their own rehabilitation facilities. The irrationality of trying to place the most chronic patients from 10% of the National Health Service's psychiatric beds into a rural and structurally flimsy hospital, miles away from the patients' homes, also became apparent. Seemingly, the regional planners of the day had not realised that most of the discharged patients would prefer to remain in Worcestershire. In 1985, the Department of Health and Social Security (DHSS) required the closure of St Wulstan's. This left behind a hard core of in-patients, as well as generations of more or less successful rehabilitees, mainly in the Malvern area. The Malvern Hills became known to some as the 'Sierra Psychotica'.

These patients also largely occupied the vocational and other places in the community, thus depriving ex-Powick patients of these facilities,

51

when they in turn needed discharge into the community. The then Unit Management Group undertook endless multidisciplinary assessments and discussion exercises for and with each individual patient. Also, every member of staff was interviewed, counselled, and considered for re-employment. There were then complex negotiations with surviving traceable relatives, as well as with often distant social-services departments and general practitioners, and this process enabled the return of at least some of these patients to their home areas. Although, in the event, the St Wulstan's closure provided a useful pilot run (and some extra nursing staff) for the closure of Powick where this process was repeated, it required such a great investment of professional time, for both health and social services, that it inevitably delayed the closure of Powick itself for some years. By 1984, there were 37 patients left at St Wulstan's who had come from large mental hospitals in the City of Birmingham, another 44 patients from other large mental hospitals in the rest of the West Midlands, two from London, and only ten patients from the Worcester Health District (Table 8.1). There was also an unknown number of highly vulnerable ex-patients who had been imported and discharged into the district since 1961. In January 1985, 54 residual in-patients were transferred to Powick Hospital.

St Wulstan's Hospital was the first mental hospital closed in this country, and Powick was the third or fourth. The catchment area of Powick comprised about 500 square miles, with a population of roughly a quarter of a

TABLE 8.1
Origins of ex-St Wulstan's patients as of 17 January 1985

Location of patients before transferred to St Wulstan's	No. of patients
Worcester District	10
All Saints' Hospital, Birmingham	5
Barnsley Hall Hospital, Bromsgrove	5
Burton Road Hospital, Dudley	2
Central Hospital, Warwick	5
Coleshill Hospital, Birmingham	3
Highcroft Hospital, Birmingham	7
Hollymoor Hospital, Birmingham	2
John Connolly Hospital, Birmingham	5
Kidderminster District	1
The Maudsley Hospital, London	1
The Midland Nerve Hospital, Birmingham	1
Monyhull Hospital, Birmingham	4
Newcross Hospital, Wolverhampton	1
Rubery Hospital, Birmingham	10
St Bernard's Hospital, London	1
St Edward's Hospital, Staffordshire	11
St George's Hospital, Staffordshire	9
St Mary's Hospital, Hereford	4
St Matthew's Hospital, Staffordshire	10
Shelton Hospital, Shrewsbury	6
Stallington Hospital, Birmingham	4

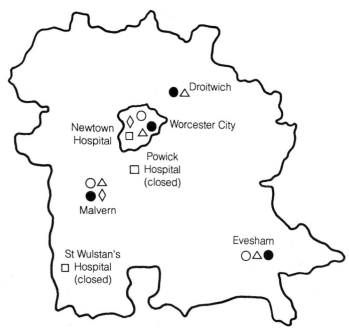

Fig. 8.1. Map showing the location of psychiatric facilities (1988) and their relationship to the big towns in Worcester Health District (◯ day hospital, △ day centre, ☐ psychiatric hospital, ● unit for elderly severely mentally infirm, ◇ hostel)

million people, and about half of this population lived in the bigger towns – Worcester, Kidderminster, Malvern, Droitwich, and Evesham (Fig. 8.1, Table 8.2). Staff and patients were initially moved into individual 'villas' within the mental hospital itself, and then to vacant staff houses on the campus, both benefiting from rehabilitation and re-education. There is a cosy metropolitan notion that tolerance for the mentally ill is much higher in non-urban areas, but what is certain is that there is a much higher intolerance of lack of service. Patients in areas such as Worcestershire, particularly those who appear to have been neglected by the health service, have a high profile, and there is a very efficient informal network to put pressure on the services for something to be done. The Malvern WHO field research centre is currently investigating the question of comparative tolerances to mental illness under the auspices of the Health Promotion Research Fund.

The new acute service

A good feature that was built into the Worcester Development Project from the start was that evaluation and research were to be carried out largely

TABLE 8.2
Origin of Powick patients

Last permanent address	No. of patients	(%)
Worcester Health District	68	50
Kidderminster Health District	22	16
Bromsgrove & Redditch Health District	3	2
West Midlands Metropolitan Districts	24	19
Warwickshire	6	4
Other English Districts	10	8
Abroad	2	1
Total	135	100

by external observers from the Medical Research Council and the University of Birmingham. Evaluations carried out on themselves by the protagonists of new projects often apparently prove whatever they happen to believe. The original intention was that Powick would cease to take admissions in 1973, with a 'closure' in 1980, the remaining 250 patients simply being dumped in Barnsley Hall Hospital, which had itself originally opened in 1907 because of overcrowding at Powick. However, this became quite unacceptable. The consultants were also originally instructed by the DHSS to 'sectorise' the population and area, but they decided against this, to allow choice to both patients and general practitioners (GPs) and to allow district-wide specialisation. Therefore, the multi-disciplinary teams are 'semi-sectorised', that is, they have non-monopoly responsibility for a particular sector. Kidderminster was originally to retain responsibility for its own patients within Powick Hospital, but this proved impracticable, and so the Worcester teams took responsibility for them. The Worcester consultants all retained personal responsibility for the residual wards at Powick, to help maintain morale – among both staff and patients. The high calibre of the nurses helped greatly.

A strategy of community psychiatric care thus developed, which can be described by using the Malvern team as an example (consultants and their teams from other sectors were of course as much involved with the closure and with development of the new service). To assume that a community necessarily harbours therapeutic or caring skills seemed a naive view. Therefore, the development started on the basis that psychiatric 'community care' meant the dispersal of care and of professional staff within a community (involving the GP and the primary-care team), but without taking for granted self-generated or non-existent community resources. It was felt that an asylum service must also be provided, but mainly on a domestic and not on an institutional scale – so far as possible, in an ordinary house in an ordinary street. All the new services were initially owned either by the health authority or by the social-services department, and no facility was closed until the appropriate new service element was opened (Table 8.3). This was necessitated by the inevitable acceleration of closure, once a point of no return

TABLE 8.3
Sequence of opening of community units

Name of establishment	Month of opening	No. of places
Rehabilitation units		
Sheffield House (Malvern)	November 1985	13
Group homes (Powick)	January 1986	13
Gregory's Mill Work Centre (Worcester)	November 1986	60
Shrubbery Avenue (Worcester)	May 1987	7
Gate House (Worcester)	October 1987	7
Cromwell House (Worcester)	November 1987	12
Stuart House (Worcester)	December 1987	11
Units for the elderly severely mentally infirm		
Hawthorns (Evesham)	March 1988	21
Rowans (Malvern)	November 1988	24
St John's (Droitwich)	December 1988	20

was reached and costs escalated. One danger resulting from this policy was of a relative exclusion of the voluntary sector, but this is now being redressed. All five hostels and three units for the elderly mentally infirm were handed over to the private/voluntary sector (e.g. the National Schizophrenia Fellowship) at the end of 1990.

Some other districts appear to have used the voluntary sector, inappropriately either for service provision or simply as an accountant's trick, whereby benefits are wrung out of non-health government funds. All the resources of the Malvern psychiatric team are always at the unquestioned command of the particular individual who is in contact with the patient, of whatever discipline or rank he/she may be. There is encouragement of the specialised and professional contribution of each discipline, to try and achieve as high professional standards as possible, without rigid demarcation of role or authority. However, if roles are made too flexible, there may be a tendency to lose high standards of professional input. Quality control and clinical audit are strongly encouraged.

So far as possible, communication within the teams is radial, not simply centripetal or centrifugal; functional team leadership has to be earned, not demanded. The concept used by the Malvern team is best likened to a spider's web: there is speed of communication, while the web as a whole maintains a reasonably organised and coherent structure. At any one time, there are two foci of leadership – one at the centre of the web and a functional one wherever a problem arises in the web; such a web is aware of individual patients and problems, and can respond quickly but flexibly. The strands of the web can be easily thickened or thinned, to provide for a patient's needs *in situ* and in a very flexible way. Patients can move easily from one part of such a service to another without delay, without loss of professional information about them, and with minimal danger of falling completely through the web. It goes without saying that the team members try to have time for each patient and the informal carers, and to involve both in carefully quantified, clearly explained, and above all precisely timed care plans and packages. Human fellow-feeling is much easier to provide in the patient's home, where the professional is a guest and where the patient is not anxious, but is in control. It is also easier for the professional to withdraw, and certain sensitivities (e.g. to the development of side-effects of neuroleptics) are much easier to detect.

A patient's inability to cope or to progress further must be tolerated, and this can be quite taxing on the team's morale. Many of the early territorial or apparent interdisciplinary disputes were in fact due to an individual staff member's lack of competence. This can be tolerated, or not even recognised in a large mental hospital, but it is all too obvious in the present type of service and represents one of its problems.

St Anne's Orchard acts as the multidisciplinary Malvern team base and as a drop-in centre, not so much for patients but for GPs and other health professionals. It also has formal out-patient clinics and is used for group therapy or self-help groups of various kinds in the evenings. It accommodates acute day patients on two days a week, elderly day patients one day, and 'rehabilitation' patients on yet another day. Until a few years ago it also acted as a hostel, so that one group of patients slept there and went out to work, while the day patients came in and went home in the evening. As the unit's activity increased and alternative hostels opened, this duality was abandoned. Recently, a multidisciplinary family-support service has been started. St Anne's often 'shares' clients with voluntary and/or social-services day centres and comprises a WHO field research centre.

The new rehabilitation service

Rehabilitation was defined by Affleck (1981) as the process by which the social disablement that accompanies or follows psychiatric disorders is identified and negated, while enabling the patient to acquire social skills, self-esteem, and confidence. This is a dynamic process, requiring active patient participation and co-operation with the multiprofessional team, since no individual staff member can ever hope to acquire all rehabilitative skills. *Resettlement* is the process by which the long-term mentally ill, through rehabilitation, are enabled to move to independent accommodation in the community, to lead as normal a life as possible there with support. Those doing best with this sort of approach are those who have been called the 'new long-stay' or 'revolving-door' patients. *Relocation* is a change of address of severely disabled people who cannot survive without continuing to receive the existing services of the psychiatric hospital unit, such as 24-hour nursing care. Those who can benefit from this process used to be called the 'old long-stay' or 'chronic' patients, previously occupying the back-wards of most mental hospitals. The new long-stay have been divided by Sheets *et al* (1982) into three groups: a 'high-functioning' group, who blend into the general population and generally have a good outcome; a 'low-energy, low-demand' group, who are passive, poorly motivated, but compliant and accepting of mental health services, and thus are easy to manage; and the 'high energy, high-demand' group, who have a very low frustration level, and frequently act out. This last group is not accepting of mental health services, and generally does rather badly. Chronicity, according to Peek & Palmer (1980), is best divided into six operational criteria: patient deficit in functioning and/or responsiveness to treatment; the presence of a dependent lifestyle; having a formal psychiatric diagnosis; the amount of time spent in psychiatric hospital; legal eligibility for financial settlement; and an indefinite need of support from services.

Armed with these definitions, we were able to divide the 'residual' Powick and St Wulstan's patients into two populations – those with early rehabilitation potential, and those without. The former were further subdivided into five groups, and relocated in our five hostels, which together provide 50 places for younger individuals who have the deficits of long-term mental illness. Some other patients live with landladies, others in housing association flats, while the most independent are in their own homes, whether council-owned or otherwise. The second, mainly elderly group (i.e. those without potential for rehabilitation) were then relocated in three units of 25 beds each, in Evesham, Malvern, and Droitwich (Table 8.3). These are basically dispersed wards, but even so are small, located in the community which they serve, for whom they offer respite care, and with which they are increasingly integrated (and 'owned').

The industrial therapy workshop in north Worcester is gradually moving from labour-intensive assembly-line work to more creative production, which has greatly benefited the people using it. Eighteen ex mental hospital patients could not leave hospital because of behavioural/social problems, and these constituted a DGH chronic ward for continuing rehabilitation in hospital. It would have been irresponsible to discharge them earlier, or perhaps ever. The recruitment of new such patients is miniscule.

The Worcester Development Project had been as handicapped as any other service by the many reorganisations within the National Health Service and by financial constraints. Nevertheless, at all times, patients and staff have been involved in open meetings with managers and clinicians, where progress with closure, opening of hostels, rationalisation of the hospital site, appointment of staff, etc., have been honestly and openly discussed. The over-riding principle has been the modest one of moving patients into at least a domestic-scale facility, and not leaving them stranded.

Evaluation

We have now reached that stage in the project when it is possible to evaluate. The case register (Chapter 12) has been invaluable in providing broad

TABLE 8.4

Total number of patient contacts per year

Year	Admissions	Attendances at out-patient department	Attendances at day hospitals	Home visits by: Consultant	Psychiatric nurse
1971	851	988	189	217	333
1977	648	1112	298	541	551
1978[1]	676	1167	486	640	601
1979[2]	801	3573	10 124	702	649
1981	823	4794	13 794	698	1747
1984	1177	5467	16 851	680	7882
1988[3]	1077	5868	25 772	753	28 020

1. Admissions to Powick ceased in 1978, with gradual run-down of beds.
2. Newtown Hospital began operating.
3. Closure of Powick, with loss of 150 remaining beds.

indicators of the use of both hospital and community services, even though between 1974 and 1978 it measured only the activities of a mental hospital preparing itself for re-siting, and between 1978 and 1986, the activities of the old plus the new services. The total number of beds nearly halved over this period, but with an increase in the number of patients being treated.

TABLE 8.5

Cost of new service

Date of opening	Name of unit	Source of funding	Cost at time of opening: £1000s	Estimated cost in 1988/89: £1000s
Expenditure				
June 1978	Kidderminster DGH		1136	2840
December 1978	Newtown DGH	WDP–RHA capital scheme	2699	6506
February 1979	Malvern day hospital		109	261
March 1979	Evesham day hospital		306	731
March 1981	Kidderminster (ESMI)	RHA capital	768	1444
September 1983	Worcester (ESMI)		1900	2717
April 1985	Powick group homes	DHA capital	380	513
November 1985	Sheffield House[1]		150	300
November 1986	Gregory's Mill		117	152
September 1987	Shrubbery Avenue[1]		146	210
November 1987	Gate[1] and Cromwell houses[1]	RHA capital scheme	278	400
December 1987	Stuart House[1]		185	240
March 1988	Hawthorn (ESMI)		260	260
November 1988	Rowans (ESMI)		429	429
December 1988	St John's (ESMI)		935	935
Total			9798	17 938
Speculated income				
	Sale of Powick site		10 000	10 000
	Sale of St Wulstan's site		1000	1000
Total				11 000

1. Ordinary houses, readily saleable on the open market at market prices. DGH, district general hospital; WDP, Worcester Development Project; RHA, regional health authority; DHA, district health authority; ESMI, elderly and severely mentally infirm.

There was also considerable growth in day-hospital and day-care activity over the corresponding periods, with greater use of other facilities, in preference to admission, in an effort to continue patients' treatments at home. The number of patient contacts by the increasing number of community nurses, for example, showed a massive rise, from 333 in 1971 to over 28 000 in 1988 (Table 8.4).

Financial evaluation is nonetheless important. The principal source of funding for the Development Project in the 1970s was the Department of Health and Social Security, which opted to 'top-slice' its total budget for this purpose, before distribution to the various regional hospital boards of that time. Funds were also available from the then Birmingham Regional Board. There is an understanding that some of this money will be repaid to the district from capital savings, land sales, etc. (Table 8.5).

It would be wrong to look at 'actual total' costs of the new facilities (£9.7 million), when the cost in today's prices is really about £17.9 million. If Kidderminster, which has developed its own services within the Kidderminster and District Health Authority, is excluded from the costs, then the gap between expenditure and incomes narrows.

The future

The majority of the mentally ill have always been cared for in and by the community from which they come. As psychiatric services become more sophisticated, there will be an ever-increasing demand for professional expertise. The peripheral day hospitals and day centres should perhaps increasingly become community mental health resource facilities, with greater emphasis on mental health, rather than entirely on mental illness. The concept of 'mental health shops' is an interesting one, and our co-operation with the voluntary sector grows apace. The service needs to continue to emphasise the importance of independence, self-reliance and self-support.

Such success as we may have had does not imply that the process can be duplicated elsewhere, since understanding of the local situation must be the key to successful planning. For those individuals who can no longer be managed in the community, in spite of maximum efforts, it is still too early to decide whether current methods of care do in fact represent a real advance. Perhaps surprisingly, the local community has given a clear, favourable mandate (Hall *et al*, 1990), but such questions as need versus demand, and many others, remain.

References

AFFLECK, J. W. (1981) The Edinburgh progressive care system. In *Handbook of Rehabilitation Practice* (eds J. K. Wing & B. Morris), pp. 151–161. Oxford: Oxford University Press.

HALL, P., BROCKINGTON, I., MURPHY, C. J., *et al* (1990) Tolerance of the mentally ill in two West Midland communities. Unpublished report to the Health Promotion Trust.

PEEK, R. & PALMER, R. R. (1980) Patients' rights and patient chronicity. *Psychiatry and the Law*, 59–71.

SHEETS, J. L., PREVOST, J. & REIHMAN, J. (1982) Young adult chronic patients: three hypothesised subgroups. *Hospital and Community Psychiatry*, **33**, 197–203.

Further reading

ABRAHAMSON, D. & BRENNER, D. (1982) Do longstay psychiatric patients want to leave hospital. *Health Trends*, **14**, 95.

BENNETT, C. (1989) The Worcester Development Project: general practitioner satisfaction with a new community psychiatric service. *Journal of the Royal College of General Practitioners*, **39**, 106–109.

CAWLEY, R. H. (1973) Postscript. In *Policy for Action* (eds R. Cawley & G. M. C. Lachlan). Oxford: Oxford University Press for the Nuffield Provincial Hospitals Trust.

CUMELLA, S. J., LAWRENCE, R. & ROBERTSON, J. A. (1988) A study of the accumulation of longstay patients in a general hospital psychiatric department. *Health Trends*, **20**, 48.

DOWRICK, C., MARKWICK, N., MARTIN, S., *et al* (1980) The Worcester experiment. *Social Work Today*, **2**, 10–15.

FALLOON, I. R. H. & PEDERSON, J. (1985) Family management in the prevention of morbidity of schizophrenia. *British Journal of Psychiatry*, **147**, 156–163.

FELDMAN, S. (1974) Community mental health centres – a decade later. *International Journal of Mental Health*, **3**, 19–34.

GUDEMAN, J. & SHORE, M. (1984) Beyond de-institutionalisation: a new class of facilities for the mentally ill. *New England Journal of Medicine*, **311**, 832–836.

HALL, P. & GILLARD, R. (1982) The Worcester Development Project. *International Journal of Social Psychiatry*, **28**, 163–172.

HASSALL, C. & ROSE, S. (1989) Powick Hospital 1979–1986: a case register study. In *Contributions to Health Service Planning and Research* (ed. J. K. Wing). London: Gaskell.

HAWKS, D. (1975) Community care – an analysis of assumptions. *British Journal of Psychiatry*, **127**, 276–285.

HOULT, J., ROSEN, A. & REYNOLDS, I. (1984) Community orientated treatment compared to psychiatric hospital orientated treatment. *Social Science and Medicine*, **18**, 1005–1010.

KHOOSAL, D. I. & JONES, P. H. (1989) Community care again: a need for definition (editorial). *Journal of the Royal Society of Medicine*, **82**, 451–452.

KORMAN, N. & GLENNISTER, H. (1985) *Closing a Hospital*. London: Bedford Square Press.

LEVENE, L. S., DONALDSON, L. J. & BRANDON, S. (1985) How likely is it that a DHA can close its large mental hospitals? *British Journal of Psychiatry*, **147**, 150–155.

LLOYD, A., MORRIS, L. N., ORAM, E. V., *et al* (1977) The Worcester Project. *Nursing Times*, **73**, 1064–1079.

PEET, M. (1986) Network community health care in N. W. Derbyshire. *Bulletin of the Royal College of Psychiatrists*, **10**, 262.

PLATT, S. D., KNIGHTS, A. C. & HIRSCH, S. R. (1980) Caution and conservation in the use of a psychiatric day hospital: evidence from a research project that failed. *Psychiatry Research*, **3**, 123–132.

RICHARDS, C. (1981) Old people and the myth of community care. *World Medicine* (April), 35–39.

STEIN, L. & TEST, M. A. (1980) Alternatives to mental hospital treatment. (i) Conceptual model, treatment program and clinical evaluation. *Archives of General Psychiatry*, **37**, 392–397.

TYRER, P. (1985) The hive system – a model for a psychiatric service. *British Journal of Psychiatry*, **146**, 571–575.

9 The Worcester Development Project 20 years on

GEORGE MILNER

At the time of the Department of Health and Social Security's (1970) feasibility study, Powick Hospital had 949 beds, of which 784 were occupied, more than half by patients over the age of 65. Its services also included out-patient facilities in six centres, day facilities, and two hostels. The study proposed separate services for Mid-Worcestershire and South Worcestershire. The planning team proposed five 30-bed wards in Worcester (based on 30 beds per 60 000 population) with only 10 day places, and two 30-bed wards in Kidderminster, with 20 day places. Day hospitals were planned in Malvern and Evesham (20 places each), plus a children's unit and an 'annexe' of 10 beds; a total of 220 day-centre places in Malvern, Worcester, Droitwich and Kidderminster as well as two hostels (in Worcester and Kidderminster) were also proposed. Geriatric facilities were to be improved, but no special provision was made for psychogeriatrics.

The adolescent and child psychiatry in-patient beds were not in fact provided, but beds for the psychiatry of old age were and residual patients from Powick were relocated in hospital hostels (rather than transferred to a neighbouring mental hospital as originally planned). The 10-bed unit was developed as an alcohol and substance abuse unit. The total number of dispersed residential places in the new service is little less than in the old mental hospital.

In 1978, some 80 patients were transferred to the new general-hospital psychiatric departments, leaving 340 patients in Powick. By 1987, 149 patients remained, including 56 who had been transferred from St Wulstan's Hospital: 70% of them were aged over 65, 40% were incapable of walking without assistance, and many were incontinent. The younger patients were often distressed by hallucinations and delusions, had chronic disabilities, and some behavioural problems.

By 1989, the population in the original Powick catchment areas had grown from 285 000 to 330 000. Worcester is numbered 146 and Kidderminster 159 (out of 192) on the Jarman Index of Social Deprivation (1983), suggesting that the area is not at all underprivileged and therefore is predicted to have

TABLE 9.1

Admission rates per 100 000 population aged 15 and over, 1983, and percentage difference 1977–83

	Rates	% difference. 1977–83
Southampton	671	+ 13
Camberwell	506	– 9
All Scotland	502	+ 5
Edinburgh	498	+ 1
Cardiff[1]	469	+ 3
Salford	442	+ 20
Aberdeen	431	– 2
Worcester	420	+ 50
All England	398	+ 6
Oxford	385	– 3

1. Cardiff, 1978–83.
Source: Wing (1989).

a low demand for psychiatric services. The number of patients in contact in 1985 was 15 000 per 100 000 population – an increase of 50% since 1974.

The admission rate in 1983 of 420 per 100 000 had also increased by 50%, when compared with 1977 (Table 9.1). Camberwell has more admissions, whereas comparable rates are found in Oxford, although their in-patient work is carried out in psychiatric hospitals (Wing, 1989). However, the median length of stay has – surprisingly – remained much the same: in 1977 it was 18½ days, and in 1983 was 19 days (Table 9.2). In Oxford, the median stays were 15 and 10 days, and in Southampton 17 and 12 days, but their admission rates for people who stay for less than one week are much higher, suggesting that more patients with milder disorders are admitted (Table 9.3). Very few people stay one to five years – about 2 per 100 000 in Worcester (Table 9.4), which compares with 24 in Camberwell and 5 in Oxford; 98% of in-patients stay less than six months – comparable with Southampton and Oxford, but more than in Camberwell or Salford.

TABLE 9.2

Median[1] length of stay (days) of patients discharged from or dying in in-patient care, 1977 and 1983, by age

	15–64		65 and over	
	1977	*1983*	*1977*	*1983*
Camberwell	41	43	70	88.5
Aberdeen	18.5	20.5	40.5	41.5
Cardiff[1]	22.5	19.4	23.3	25.6
Salford	19.6	19.7	40	37
Worcester	18.5	19.1	29.5	25
Edinburgh	20	18	40	23
Southampton	17	12	23	19.5
Oxford	15	10	20	14

1. Cardiff 1978–83.
Source: Wing (1989).

TABLE 9.3
Percentage of in-patients discharged or dying in 1983, by length of stay

	Less than 1 week			Less than 1 month			Less than 6 months		
	15–64	65 and over	15 and over	15–64	65 and over	15 and over	15–64	65 and over	15 and over
Camberwell	11	6	10	38	24	35	90	68	85
Aberdeen	16	5	13	63	32	54	93	68	86
Edinburgh	19	7	15	67	58	64	95	87	92
Worcester	20	10	16	74	60	69	98	89	95
Salford	22	7	17	69	46	61	95	80	89
Cardiff	25	10	20	66	60	64	96	84	92
Southampton	34	6	21	79	70	75	97	95	96
Oxford	37	9	27	73	73	73	97	91	95

Source: Wing (1989).

The combined Worcester and Kidderminster services, which are now well established, have 492 whole-time-equivalent nurses, 21 qualified or assistant occupational therapists, 11 staff doctors, 15 psychiatrists in training, 8 psychologists, some seconded social workers, and 60 managerial and administrative staff. This contrasts with the staffing structure in 1968, when 282 whole-time-equivalent nurses were employed, 25 qualified or assistant occupational therapists, 4 staff doctors, 4 trainee psychiatrists, 9 social workers, 12 mental welfare officers, 26 administrative staff, and 2 psychologists.

The total revenue expenditure is some £11.2 million per annum, at 1988 prices. This includes the revenue costs of both the Worcester and Kidderminster services (£7.5 million), the cost of the relocated Powick patients (£3 million) – including the resettled elderly patients – and the costs to the social services (£0.7 million). If Powick had continued to provide psychiatric services as before, the estimated revenue cost at 1988 prices would be some £5 million per annum. Any reduction in revenue expenditure

TABLE 9.4
Resident in-patients, 31 December 1983, by length of stay and age – rates per 100 000 total population

	Length of stay in years, by age group											
	15–64				65 and over				15 and over			
	<1	1–5	5 and over	Total	<1	1–5	5 and over	Total	<1	1–5	5 and over	Total
Camberwell	71	24	25	120	40	33	47	120	111	57	72	241
Salford	35	22	41	98	29	44	60	133	64	66	102	231
Cardiff	33	13	25	71	30	28	35	92	63	40	59	163
Southampton	29	13	23	65	30	17	18	65	59	30	41	130
Worcester	20	2	17	39	23	13	34	71	43	15	52	110
Oxford	21	5	6	32	17	12	11	40	38	17	18	72
England	29	12	23	65	27	24	31	82	56	36	55	147
Wales	30	12	25	67	28	23	32	82	59	34	57	150
Aberdeen	41	28	35	103	50	64	50	165	91	92	85	268
Scotland	42	26	49	118	48	59	77	184	91	85	126	302

Source: Wing (1989).

will depend upon how many 'hump' facilities (i.e. those services provided for the resettled Powick and St Wulstan's patients) continue to be used by new generations of patients. A further reduction of costs to the Health Service for these patients could be achieved by entering into arrangements with the voluntary sector (Department of Health and Social Security, 1983, 1984). The capital costs involved were some £17.5 million, at 1989 prices. The sale of Powick Hospital site is expected to realise some £10 million, but the St Wulstan's site cannot be sold at present, because of a restrictive covenant.

Discussion

There has been no sudden, dramatic change in the pattern of clinical services; what changes there have been have occurred gradually. More patients are being treated, and those in treatment are using more services. The median in-patient stay of patients is short and so far, the accumulation of 'new long-stay' is negligible. This does not appear to be due to a drift of patients away to other areas.

A project like this must stand or fall by the quality of care given to patients. A working party of the Royal College of Psychiatrists equated quality of care with activity, efficiency, and efficacy in providing treatment at the level of the current state of psychiatric knowledge (Hirsch, 1988). Activity and efficiency are easily measured, and continue to increase in the Worcester Development Project, but efficacy is difficult to monitor in a widely dispersed service, staffed by several independent professions.

The House of Commons Social Services Committee (1988) suggested that every patient leaving hospital should have a carefully prepared treatment plan to optimise quality of life. This is accepted practice in the Worcester Development Project, but many patients may receive treatment in several settings, from a variety of professionals. There is some danger, therefore, of duplication or undue overlap of services. Targeting of resources towards the relatively milder forms of illness, at the expense of severe illness, can also occur unless there is careful co-ordination and interdisciplinary agreement.

The closure and replacement of a mental hospital is a complex and lengthy business. There will be a 'hump' timespan, during which there will be a need to support two services. Our new service is not cheaper, but I believe it is better.

Acknowledgement

Christine Hassall kindly provided data from the Worcester Case Register.

References

DEPARTMENT OF HEALTH AND SOCIAL SECURITY (1970) *Worcester Development Project: Feasibility Study for a Model Reorganisation of Mental Illness Services* MO(M1)56. London: HMSO.

—— (1983) *Care in the Community and Joint Finance* (HC(83)6) (LAC(83)5). Heywood (Lancashire): Department of Health and Social Security.

—— (1984) *Voluntary Organisation Representation on Joint Consultative Committees and Extension of the Joint Finance Arrangements* (HC(84)9) (LAC(84)8). Heywood (Lancashire): Department of Health and Social Security.

HIRSCH, S. R. (1988) *Psychiatric Beds and Resources: Factors Influencing Bed Use and Service Planning*, London: Gaskell.

HOUSE OF COMMONS SOCIAL SERVICES COMMITTEE (1988) *Community Care: Agenda for Action. A Report to the Secretary of State for Social Services*. London: HMSO.

JARMAN, B. (1983) Identification of underprivileged areas. *British Medical Journal*, **246**, 1705–1709.

WING, J. K. (ed.) (1989) *Contribution to Health Services Planning and Research: Comparative Studies from Psychiatric Case Registers*. London: Gaskell.

10 Professional perspectives on the Worcester Development Project

**ROBIN STEEL, DAVID TOMBS,
SIMON HODGSON, A. NEIL CHAPMAN
and JAMES C. WAITS**

*The general practitioner:
Robin Steel*

What did general practitioners (GPs) think of Powick Hospital? How were they involved in the planning of the Worcester Development Project? What do GPs think of the change, and what do they hope for in the future? There are 119 GPs in Worcester District in 31 practices.

When giving opinions under Section 12 of the Mental Health Act, I visit the psychiatric unit at Newtown Hospital frequently (as in the past, I went to Powick Hospital). I have also been a police surgeon, am secretary of the Local Medical Committee, and am a general practitioner in Worcester itself, thus giving me a comprehensive perspective of the psychiatric service. My father was also a GP in the town from 1931 to 1982, and was on the Powick Management Committee at the beginning of the National Health Service.

Powick Hospital appeared to me to be a very progressive mental hospital. The consultants of the 1950s and 1960s offered good out-patient services, much valued by GPs. There was also an emergency service, where the patient could be sent to the hospital, be seen within the hour, and admitted immediately if necessary; this is more difficult in the new-style service.

How were GPs involved in planning the changes? We were involved in the original consultations and had representation on the co-ordinating committee. One example of our contribution was that we believed the original feasibility study had vastly under-rated the need for psychogeriatric provision. A survey of our psychogeriatric patients in Worcester District confirmed this, and the Elgar Unit was subsequently built, partly at least as the result of pressure from us.

On the whole, general practitioners now think the scheme a very good one (Bennett, 1989). As an adviser to the National Schizophrenia Fellowship, I have told that body about the service that we receive in Worcester District and about the co-operation GPs get from consultants and others; the Fellowship wishes similar schemes existed elsewhere.

Between October 1983 and July 1985, Bennett (1989) approached 161 general practitioners in the Kidderminster and Worcester Health Districts, and interviewed 88% of them. Only a fifth had had any training in psychiatry or were interested in psychiatry, over and above their general practice interest. Out of the 161, all but 14 were pleased on the whole with the new service, and the 14 who were not expressed dissatisfaction in one or two specific areas, which flavoured their overall impression. Some felt that there were sometimes problems in communication. For instance, a social worker at the day centre, seeing a single-parent mother who has been attending there all week, phones on Friday evening to say that the patient's depression is worsening, and would I do something about it? By the time I have arranged a domiciliary visit and she has been admitted, I will not get home until 9.30 p.m. There are also problems of the interface between psychiatric illness, mental handicap, and child psychiatry that have not been adequately grasped.

Nevertheless, local GPs feel that patients are getting a better service, even though they themselves have to work harder than in the past. For example, the case register shows that each practice was only referring one or two depressive patients annually to a psychiatrist in 1985. Yet the volume of antidepressants prescribed shows clearly that we were dealing with larger numbers of such patients.

The majority of new entrants to local general practice have passed through vocational training locally. They thus spend six months in psychiatry, and they vote this as the subject that is best taught (which says much for our consultant psychiatrists). In the future, though, I would like to see better communication about such matters as when patients are attending day care or when they have ceased to do so.

The County Council's Director of Social Services: David Tombs

'Care in the community' is a term which currently dominates the lives of all involved in the caring professions. On the one hand, there are projects that reflect a determination to offer appropriate services to people in need, and that focus on what must be paramount for success –

services which enshrine recognition of the rights of the individual, aiming to uphold that person's dignity in all circumstances. On the other, there are attitudes which hanker after the status quo and where movement is perhaps more appropriately measured in terms which are akin to geological time.

In Worcester, in the late 1960s and the 1970s, the impetus was launched towards this new era of care in the community. Initially, it had every advantage, with promises of detailed and co-ordinated planning, multi-agency involvement, adequate resources, and the machinery to ensure completion. Yet we who have been participants have to recognise that while we have made much progress, we have not realised all the ambitions of those heady early days.

It was necessary to demonstrate at the outset that the various professionals could work together on the planning of services and on the implementation of those plans. To do this, a co-ordinating committee was established, providing a platform from which we could in fact work together. However, there were over 40 people on that committee. Only three represented the local authority: a lawyer, a housing manager, and myself as the Director of Social Services. The other members were from the health services in local, central, or academic guise. From the inception of the Project in 1969 to the ultimate closure of Powick Hospital in 1989 was a long time. If this pattern were to be demonstrated elsewhere, it would not be surprising if national policy-makers became impatient and sought other solutions which might not prove at all successful.

It was really the willingness of government to put forward finance for development that enabled the different agencies to work together. No one could have predicted the national financial problems in the mid-1970s, which led to cutbacks then and subsequently. Progress has, however, been maintained both in the provision of facilities and of professional time. It has meant that the local authority has had to absorb increased costs from the psychiatric service, at a time when other budgets were reducing. I can hardly boast, however, about the fact that only 3% of the social-services budget in Hereford or Worcester is spent on services for mentally ill people.

Partnership is the important concept in working together. It implies equality, but within the hospital world, the medically qualified have traditionally been given the status of overlords, and this is carrying forward into community work. However, it is often the social workers who tend to seek participation based on clients' self-determination. It can be a struggle for those working together in a team to reconcile giving up power to the client; if the team is not able to cope with these confrontations, or to understand each others' values, then the prognosis has to be poor for that team and for the people the team is intending to help.

In this process of developing partnerships, housing authorities (district councils, housing associations and the voluntary sector) have a significant part to play. Closer involvement by mental health professionals in these activities gives a far greater opportunity for influencing their decisions. Similarly, involvement of such vital people as landladies can dramatically influence the lives of the people we are attempting to help. One cannot ignore the vital role of carers in partnership with us: we know that the vast majority of those suffering from a psychiatric illness are dependent on those who care for them. We know how often it is the carer who is under greatest stress.

I believe that we were remiss in failing to insist at the outset on more comprehensive research into the consequences of what we were doing in this Project, and regret that we were unable to achieve a jointly agreed research programme on the quality of its outcome. It has always amazed me that central government could have invested so much into the Project without regarding it as essential from the outset that such research was a vital ingredient. We must now demonstrate that through closely working together, we can achieve the best with what we have. Then, we can set out what more is required, which can only be realised through the injection of further resources. Community care is a very complex subject, but I suspect that full realisation of this has only recently dawned in Whitehall.

The mental health unit general manager: Simon Hodgson

I found myself appointed in the mid-1980s as the general manager of a unit that was really two units and not one. One was based on the new services at Newtown General Hospital, with a web of services springing out from there, and another network of services was based at Powick. Until then, there had been a third unit, at St Wulstan's Hospital, where the philosophy was utterly different from that at Powick, with a totally different medical leadership. The segments of the service were so different that many staff did not know those staff in the other units. Powick still had 170 patients, some of them originating from St Wulstan's and others having been there for many years.

There was low morale at Powick, voiced in phrases such as: "We're going to close," "We don't really believe we ever will. They've been saying we're going to close for so many years now, and we've not heard a thing about when, so we don't really think we ever will. It may happen one day, but we don't believe it." There was also a lack of direction and there was lethargy, among both staff and patients.

The worst thing about telling staff that the hospital was going to close was the implicit message that they were not needed any more. They therefore began to think that perhaps there was something wrong with the way they had provided the service. It was very hard to convince people that the future change was based upon the excellence of the past.

However, there was a series of managerial initiatives, including a 'task force', which consisted of regional officers, district officer, consultants, and a variety of other interested people. Its objectives were: firstly, to work out a future which all those different types of people could share in and agree, whatever level and professional background they came from; secondly, to get the patients out; thirdly, to decide how we would provide the new style of service; and fourthly, to decide how to finance it. The last objective was the most difficult one.

That task force was in turn supported by a network of other activities. A 'Powick relocation team' worked out the practicalities of what the task force had previously decided in theoretical terms. There was also a series of levels of consultation: a joint consultative committee and meetings with union shop stewards; monthly staff meetings; and the unit management group, consisting of managers, clinicians, a nurse, and a general practitioner. Much had fortunately been learnt from the preceding closure of St Wulstan's.

One of the first things the task force did was to ask: what sorts of patients are in Powick at the moment, and how can we relocate them? It was concluded that in broad terms, the patients fell into two categories: the elderly mentally ill and the others – they could go into premises that one day would become rehabilitating services – though in fact it might only be possible to improve their condition a little. The relocation team examined each patient's situation in detail and were fortunate in the quality of previous numerous assessments, not only by clinicians, nurses, and social workers, but by the Medical Research Council's research team.

In many ways, it would have been better to keep Powick running and at the same time start the new service, but that was impossible, for reasons of both finance and morale. We then calculated what it would cost to run the service after the closure of Powick, if we were given the premises that were needed. If that was done £1.3 million per annum could be returned to the regional health authority, so that for every month of delay, another £100 000 was lost. This clarified the minds of everyone very quickly and the whole process moved at an unprecedented speed.

At Powick, I saw concern for the patients, fear and anger. Staff felt fear because they were not sure what the future was for them. They felt anger because there was this unstated premise that because we wanted to change, the past must be wrong, and that was their fault. Concern for their patients was perhaps the most real of all. In talking about the new service, hospital staff have been reduced to tears, not because of their own fear for the future, but because they had a genuine interest in the welfare of the patients that they had served for so many years. Almost all the staff jumped to wrong conclusions, both about the future service and about the appointments that were to be arranged in the new service. There were particular unexpected problems, with mischievously leaked documents giving wrong impressions. That was a very serious management problem which others may have to face.

Those obtaining posts in the new organisation would have to show that they would be able to lead the service in that direction, and not in the direction they had gone in before. I made the decision that I would tell staff so quite openly. The total number of trained staff needed would be the same as in the old service, but not all could remain as sisters or charge nurses. There was a major problem, in that we had far too many nursing assistants. This produced grievances and difficulties in making appointments, but it also gave advantages. The main advantage was that the staff realised that many of them would have to find work elsewhere, and had between 18 months and two years to do it in, not just a matter of weeks. Fortunately, other unit managers in the district were willing to appoint those people to posts in their units, and that lessened difficulties with redundancies from Powick. That particularly traumatic period came to an end almost immediately after the appointments to the new service were made. Then, there was a new energy, a disappearance of low morale, and a new direction to the service.

Patients and staff were moved so that they could transfer smoothly to the new accommodation. The closure of one building block at Powick released £100 000 in heating and cleaning costs. This enabled us to pay for furniture, equipment, training and other things that were needed to go ahead. We had also to examine other services that were coincidentally on the Powick site – laundry, linen, sewing room, works department, catering department, which served other units as well as Powick. There was also the district training department and ambulance control.

In conclusion, although some staff have unfortunately not been able to make the change, the feeling has generally been that the new facilities, the new premises, and the new style of service are much improved.

Treasurer of the District Health Authority: Neil Chapman

I have done much agonising over what should be the funding policy for mental health services. There seem to have been four prerequisites for our relatively successful outcome. The first is that there were no new admissions to Powick Hospital since 1978, a gap of 11 years between the last admission and closure in 1989. This time-scale allowed the retention of funds that had been formerly spent on patients who died during this period, to finance the new service.

The second prerequisite was that the Department of Health and Social Security (DHSS) put in extra resources. The costs of running the new service always exceeded the savings made at Powick. Between 1981/82 and 1987/88, about £3.5 million per annum was supplied to ease the change-over from the old service to the new. Since the closure of Powick, early in 1989, however, the allocation has been reduced by £2 million. This means that in real terms, the Worcester Development Project costs £1.5 million more per annum than the old Powick institutional service, representing a 20% increase in revenue costs. Capital money was advanced for new facilities and the combined cost of those is, in 1989 prices, around £15 million, which far exceeds the expected proceeds from the sale of the Powick site. We think that the new service is worth a 20% increase in costs, but the funding has come with the Project.

The third prerequisite for a successful outcome is a common-sense financial deal. The regional health authority was willing to allow the district to keep its underspendings at Powick Hospital for the last two or three years before closure, and bank that money with them; this amounted to £1.25 million. There are between 40 and 50 ex-Powick patients in community units for whom revenue does not exist in the long term, so that in the next six or seven years, that sum will have to be drawn on to finance the shortfall.

The fourth prerequisite is to have a demonstrably good service as a legacy. Spending on psychiatric services as a percentage of total spending in the average district, regionally and nationally, is around 12½%. However, the Worcester District spends something like 17½% of its total resources on psychiatric services, even after the loss of the £2 million from its allocation, following the closure of Powick. So we spend about £1½ million more than average on psychiatric services, and it is my impression that this is accounted for largely by medical staffing, psychogeriatric beds and day facilities, and by the community psychiatric nursing service.

However, not everything in the garden is rosy. Because 50 ex-Powick patients are currently 'blocking' the rehabilitation facilities, there will effectively be no rehabilitation service until the number of these patients falls below 27, which is the long-term affordable provision. If the new allocation to Worcester and District Health Authority, following "Working for Patients", the 1989 white paper on reform of the Health Service, is purely on a capitation basis, with no allowance for protecting psychiatric services, then it will be approximately £1½ million less than present costs. Then, a decision would have to be made whether to continue protecting psychiatric services financially and whether we could afford to do so.

My first ingredient in a 'recipe for disaster' for closing a hospital would be trying to do it in too little time. Districts would then have to pay other agencies for taking patients, which could not be done without extra resources. The district's own growth money could be used, but there are other needs to be met, such as fully funding pay awards. In the Worcester Development Project area, income-support payments are being received from social services for 80 patients, amounting to around £250 000 a year.

A second ingredient would be a prescriptive funding policy. The policy in the West Midlands Region is that hospitals give the average cost of a patient to his/her home district, which then has a choice. It can continue to buy the service from the hospital where the patient already resides, or it can put this funding towards the cost of community care, yet knowing that it will not be enough.

Poor outcomes also result from patients who have been placed in semi-independent accommodation, but then deteriorate clinically, and the district is then not able to fund their intensive care. Whatever it is, a formal funding policy is merely a way of avoiding disputes: only extra money ensures a successful outcome. If the proceeds of the sale of mental hospitals were 'ring-fenced', so that they could not be used for non-psychiatric purposes, the capital obtained from them might make new community services financially viable.

A final ingredient is a community service providing a service for only half the patients, at a greater cost than the old service, with patients 'falling through the gaps'. So far, Worcester appears to have been able to avoid that, but it is not a cheap option.

General Manager of the District Health Authority: James C. Waits

Annoyingly for those who worked in general acute services, it was decided that the first phase of Worcester's new district general hospital should be for psychiatric care. It had always been the tradition in the National Health Service that the first phase of any hospital development should provide for general acute services, not psychiatric services. The Department of Health's expectation was that a new service and its supporting facilities in the community would be self-financing from the money that would come from the long-stay hospital's closure and eventual sale.

Initially, it was proposed that 120 residual patients would transfer to an alternative mental hospital. It had been estimated that the number of patients in Powick would reduce by 9% a year, and that estimate proved to be remarkably accurate. The district management team therefore expected the date of closure to be about 1992. By 1982, it was realised that it would not be possible to transfer those 120 patients elsewhere, and worse, that no coherent plans had so far been made for the constructive run-down of the mental hospital.

As patients died, so the number of buildings that were needed was reduced. The unit administrator had been able to achieve a reduction in the number of wards in use, to the point where one of the main building blocks was empty. It was argued by some that they should knock down these buildings, to save costs, but the then area team of officers refused to agree, and we were lucky that that decision was taken.

In 1983, the new district health authority decided to try to close another large psychiatric hospital also in the Malvern Hills, St Wulstan's. This had been tried in the late 1970s, but the proposal was rejected by the Secretary of State at that time. It was realised that the patients in that hospital could be transferred to the empty buildings at Powick Hospital, saving substantial sums of money. After an acrimonious period of consultation, it was agreed that 54 patients should in fact be transferred to Powick Hospital.

In 1985, the Health Advisory Service said that the remaining patients in Powick should be transferred to accommodation in the community, without further delays. Staff would be increasingly difficult to recruit to hospitals which had no future, while the increased value of the old hospital sites made a capital investment to transfer the patients more practicable than before. In 1986, the regional and district health authorities set up a joint task force to plan the closure of Powick Hospital: one of its first tasks was to prepare a new mental health strategy, which identified the levels of service that would be needed, both in the short term and in the long term. It was then obvious that more accommodation would be needed in the community initially, than in the longer term. The needs of the patients were individually assessed by multidisciplinary teams. The possibility was considered of transferring about 90 of the 150 remaining patients into a private nursing home for the elderly mentally ill, but there were difficulties, particularly with the trade unions. Eventually, it was concluded that the patients should be transferred into large houses, where they could live in groups of between three and twelve.

The inevitably accelerating speed of closure, once the mental hospital population had reduced beyond a critical point, was such that this had to be done belatedly, compared with some other districts, which had not been faced with major closures, but only by the need to develop new services. What we have learnt from this experience is that more planning should have been done at an earlier stage, and it is to be hoped that others will learn from our errors.

Reference

BENNETT, C. (1989) The Worcester Development Project. General practitioner satisfaction with the new psychiatric service. *Journal of the Royal College of General Practitioners*, **39**, 106–119.

11 The impact of community care on the course of schizophrenia in Kidderminster

ROBIN E. LAWRENCE

Kidderminster General Hospital (KGH) has a catchment area of some 99 000 in North Worcestershire (and also serves an isolated part of South Shropshire, with a population of 12 000) with 30 beds for adult mental illness. During the first six years of operation there were 607 patients admitted from the community on 1149 occasions. On the seventh anniversary of opening there were only three who had been in hospital continuously for over 12 months and only four others who were in continuing care elsewhere. Over the seven years there had been no accumulation of the new long-stay patients (NLS – any patients staying more than a year) and a major factor accounting for this was the low number of patients suffering from schizophrenia who had stayed over six months. A total of 24 patients (of that six-year cohort) had, at some time during the seven years, been in-patients (in any hospital) for more than six months and only five of these had a diagnosis of schizophrenia. This finding is in marked contrast to the world literature, which describes the following rates of NLS: 7–8/100 000 per year (Hafner & Klug, 1982) (Mannheim, Germany), 39/100 000 per four-year period (Wing & Hailey, 1972) (Camberwell, London), and Mann & Cree (1976) found that 1.9% of all admissions became long stay and reported a prevalence of 50/100 000 who had been in hospital for over 12 months, 44% of whom had schizophrenia.

I investigated the apparent lack of chronic schizophrenia in Kidderminster, exploring the following hypotheses.

(a) There is an unusually low incidence of schizophrenia in Kidderminster.
(b) Schizophrenia in Kidderminster has an unusually high mortality.
(c) Schizophrenic patients from Kidderminster are receiving long-stay care in other facilities (nearby mental hospitals, prison, etc.).
(d) Schizophrenic patients are living with relatives or friends who are under considerable stress.
(e) Schizophrenic patients are living alone, neglected and in squalor.
(f) Schizophrenic patients rotate between home and hospital, with substantial periods in hospital equivalent to long stay.

TABLE 11.1
Comparison of Barnsley Hall Hospital and Kidderminster General Hospital

	Barnsley Hall Hospital 1978–84/85	Kidderminster Hospital 1978–84/85
Comparison of hospitals		
Population served	125 000	111 000
Rank on Jarman scale (out of 165)	124	159
Average no. of consultants	2.2	1.8
Average no. of junior doctors	2.5	4.0
Average no. of clinical psychologists	0.4	2.5
Average no. of social workers	1.5	2.0
Average no. of CPNs	2.5	4.0
No. of acute beds	35	30
No. of long-stay beds	20	0
No. of day-hospital places	13	50
No. of industrial therapy places	25	0
No. of day-centre places	0	60
No. of rehabilitation hostel places	0	12
No. of group-home places	9	3
Median length of admissions: days	31	14
Cumulative lengths of stays: no. of patients		
more than 1 year	46	17
more than 2 years	18	7
Comparison of patients		
No. of patients admitted from community	482	607
No. previously admitted	398	544
No. meeting diagnostic criteria of three schemes	83	62
No. with no evidence of schizophrenia on any system	35	12
No. of schizophrenic patients found on further searching	1	1
No. of schizophrenics/schizoaffectives followed up	49	51
No. who could not be found	6	3
No. who refused to take part	4	2
No. dead	2	1
No. on whom interviews were completed	37	45
Social circumstances at follow-up		
Gross neglect	1	0
Some neglect	5	4
Satisfactory	20	18
Comfortable	11	23
Living alone	3	12
Living with family	31	30
Living in hostel	1	1
Living in hospital	2	2
Incidence of schizophrenia per 100 000 per year		
DSM–III	3.46	3.45
ICD–10	4.13	4.35
RDC	4.58	4.8

(g) Better treatment and rehabilitation leads to those suffering from schizophrenia no longer needing long hospital stays.

In order to explore these possibilities the nearest equivalent socio-demographic area (Jarman, 1983, 1984) with a dissimilar psychiatric service was chosen. That service (Barnsley Hall Hospital – BHH) was compared with Kidderminster's on a number of parameters (Table 11.1). If the percentages of patients having different cumulative lengths of hospital stay are plotted, the average patient is found to stay twice as long in BHH as KGH and, as shown in Fig. 11.1, this is true over the entire distribution of lengths of stay for all the patients. Half the patients admitted

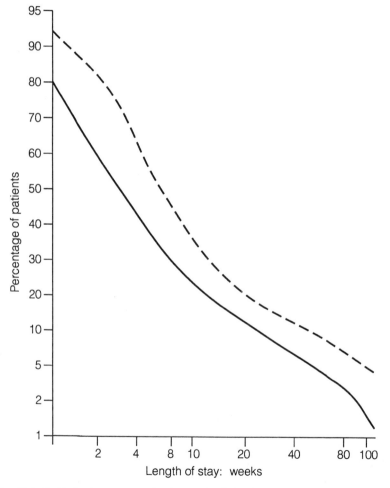

Fig. 11.1. Graph showing percentage of patients staying in hospital by length of stay (――― KGH, ----- *BHH)*

TABLE 11.2
The coefficient of agreement between diagnostic systems for 145 cases (Cohen's kappa)

	DSM–III	ICD–10
RDC	0.57	0.65
DSM–III	—	0.73

to KGH spent less than three weeks in hospital over the seven years while more than half the patients admitted to BHH spent over six weeks as in-patients, and while only 5% of Kidderminster patients have spent more than 40 weeks in hospital, over 10% of BHH patients spent more than 40 weeks as in-patients in the same period.

To compare the patients suffering from schizophrenia I reviewed all the case notes looking for patients with possible, broadly defined schizophrenia. The 145 case notes selected were subjected to a polydiagnostic procedure (Brockington *et al*, 1978) with the consultant in charge of the case as an independent co-rater. The Research Diagnostic Criteria (RDC; Spitzer *et al*, 1978), DSM–III (American Psychiatric Association, 1980), and ICD–10 (World Health Organization, 1989) were the criteria applied and good inter-rater (Cohen's kappa = 0.6–0.8) and concordance were attained (Table 11.2).

All new patients conforming to any schizophrenic or schizoaffective diagnosis in any system who were first diagnosed between 1978 and 1984 were identified and followed up in 1987–88. The patients, their nearest relative or 'important other', and their professional key worker were interviewed. It took about one and a half days per patient. As shown in Table 11.1, 88% of the KGH cohort and nearly 76% of the BHH cohort were interviewed. There were 23 DSM–III definite schizophrenic patients identified in KGH and 26 DSM–III definite schizophrenic patients identified in BHH; of these one refused interview from Kidderminster and two refused and one had died from BHH. Thus 22 DSM–III schizophrenic and 23 non-DSM–III schizophrenic patients were followed up from KGH and 23 DSM–III schizophrenic and 14 non-DSM–III schizophrenic patients were followed up from BHH.

By closely comparing the course of schizophrenia when treated in these two different services it was hoped to identify in what ways treatment style and setting affected outcome as judged by:

(a) length of stay
(b) positive and negative symptoms, assessed using the Present State Examination (PSE; Wing *et al*, 1974) and the Krawiecka Scale (Krawiecka *et al*, 1978)
(c) social function, assessed using the Social Functioning Schedule (short version with the patient and long version with the nearest relative) and the Social and Behavioural Assessment Schedule (Platt *et al*, 1980) with the professional key worker

(d) patient and nearest relative's satisfaction with the service received
(e) the General Health Questionnaire (GHQ; Goldberg, 1972) to assess general levels of psychiatric morbidity in both the patient and the nearest relative
(f) burden on the relative, assessed using the (unpublished) Medical Research Council's Self Rating Burden Questionnaire
(g) the nearest relative's perception of the patient's handicap, assessed together with a global measure of the relative's and the patient's social circumstances at follow-up.

The results showed that fewer patients per head of the population were admitted to BHH (0.64 per 1000 per year compared with 0.91 per 1000 per year to KGH) and in this way BHH had a higher threshold to both admission and discharge than KGH. Or, to put it another way, KGH was much more a part of the community it served that BHH in that the boundary between it and the outside population was much more fluid. The incidence of schizophrenia in the two areas was identical (see Table 11.1) and there was no excess of deaths in the community-treated patients. I found no evidence of drift, 'dumping', neglect or 'revolving-door' patients in either area and there were no significant differences between the two groups in social functioning, positive or negative symptoms, social circumstances, physical health, the assessed burden on the nearest relative, or the relative's satisfaction with the service. Differences within the groups were greater than those between the two hospitals on all measures including length of stay (KGH mean 135 days, BHH 155 days). If, however, DSM–III schizophrenia is excluded from both groups, then (although the numbers are small) patients stayed in KGH for a significantly shorter time than in BHH and had better outcomes on all measures. This important finding suggests that DSM–III (or core Kreapelinian) schizophrenia is much less responsive to environmental change (is less plastic) than is sometimes thought. There is, in effect, a bedrock of 'process' which, no matter how good the community service, will continue to need old-style asylum care in a sheltered, highly staffed environment. Improving community services may well reduce the number of core cases graduating to this level of dependency, but in this study that core was large enough to render all differences in outcome measures between the two services statistically insignificant.

Acknowledgements

I am pleased to acknowledge the financial support of the West Midlands Regional Health Authority which funded me as a Sheldon Fellow for two years and Dr M. Beedie, Dr D. McGovern, and Dr J. Robertson for their collaboration and access to their patients.

References

AMERICAN PSYCHIATRIC ASSOCIATION (1980) *Diagnostic and Statistical Manual of Mental Disorders* (3rd edn) (DSM–III). Washington, DC: APA.

BROCKINGTON, I. F., KENDELL, R. E. & LEFF, J. P. (1978) Definitions of schizophrenia, concordance and prediction of outcome. *Psychological Medicine*, **8**, 387–398.

GOLDBERG, D. P. (1972). *The Detection of Psychiatric Illness by Questionnaire.* London: Oxford University Press.

HAFNER, H. & KLUG, J. (1982) The impact of an expanding community mental health service on patterns of bed usage; evaluation of a four-year pattern of implementation. *Psychological Medicine*, **12**, 782–785.

JARMAN, B. (1983) Identification of underprivileged areas. *British Medical Journal*, **268**, 1705–1709.

—— (1984) Validation and distribution of scores. *British Medical Journal*, **289**, 1587–1592.

KRAWIECKA, M., GOLDBERG, D. & VAUGHAN, M. (1977) A standardised assessment scale for rating chronic psychiatric patients. *Acta Psychiatrica Scandinavica*, **55**, 299–308.

MANN, S. A. & CREE, W. (1976) 'New' long stay psychiatric patients: a national sample survey of fifteen mental hospitals in England and Wales. *Psychological Medicine*, **6**, 603–616.

PLATT, S. D., NETMAN, A. J., HIRSCH, S. R., *et al* (1980) The Social Behaviour Assessment Schedule (SBAS): rationale, contents, scoring and reliability of a new interview schedule. *Social Psychiatry*, **15**, 43–55.

SPITZER, R. L., ENDICOTT, J. & ROBINS, E. (1978) Research Diagnostic Criteria: rationale and reliability. *Archives of General Psychiatry*, **38**, 1250–1258.

WING, J. K. & HAILEY, A. M. (1972) *Evaluating a Community Psychiatric Service.* London: Oxford University Press.

——, COOPER, J. E. & SARTORIUS, N. (1974) *The Measurement and Classification of Psychiatric Symptoms.* London: Cambridge University Press.

WORLD HEALTH ORGANIZATION (1989) *International Classification of Diseases*, 10th revision, draft of Chapter V. Geneva: WHO.

12 The Worcester Psychiatric Case Register

CHRISTINE HASSALL

The Worcester Psychiatric Case Register was set up by the Department of Health and Social Security (DHSS) as an integral part of the Worcester Development Project. It contains a computerised record of all patients in the psychiatric services from 1 January 1973 until its closure in February 1987, when the Worcester District felt unable to continue financing it.

The register was set up to provide a database for the in-house research team, funded by the DHSS, and mental health professionals. Annual reports (containing non-confidential material) were circulated throughout the Development Project area. Particulars of patients that were recorded included sex, date of birth, civil state, area of residence, family doctor, and primary and secondary psychiatric diagnoses. Details of the recording of services are shown in Table 12.1. From these data, it is possible to build up a longitudinal history for each patient, from the date of entry into the psychiatric services.

TABLE 12.1
Method of recording case register data

Item of service	Data recorded
In-patient admission	Date of admission, date of discharge, in-patient identifier code
Out-patient appointment	Date of appointment, out-patient clinic identifier code
Day-hospital attendance	Start date, end date, number of attendances per month, day-hospital identifier code
Local authority day-centre attendance	As for day hospital
Domiciliary visit by psychiatrist	Date of visit
Contact with: community psychiatric nurse	Number of contacts per month, nurse-team identifier code
social worker	Number of contacts per month
psychologist	Date of contact
Residence in group home	Start date, end date
Residence in psychiatric hostel	Start date, end date, hostel identifier code

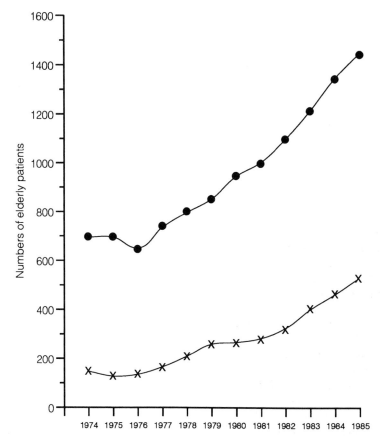

Fig. 12.1. An example of the use of the psychiatric case register comparing the number of all elderly patients (aged 65 and over) in the district (●———●) with those with dementia (✗———✗)

Some of our findings from a recent study of the elderly in the psychiatric services (Fig. 12.1) serve to demonstrate the use of the register.

A contact day is defined as a day when the patient was in touch with the services, for example, a day's residence in hospital or a day when a community nurse made a visit. In 1974 the total number of service days delivered was just over 21 000; by 1985 this had risen to 172 000. The mean number of contact days per patient receiving care appears to have stabilised at about 40 days per year.

One of the aims of the Project was to provide services that are easily accessible and available for all patients, and there has been a trend towards patients using more services (Fig. 12.2).

The contribution of local-authority social services to the care of the mentally ill has also increased since the introduction of the Register (Fig. 12.3). If, as with some registers, the use made of social services by patients was not recorded, this information would have been lost.

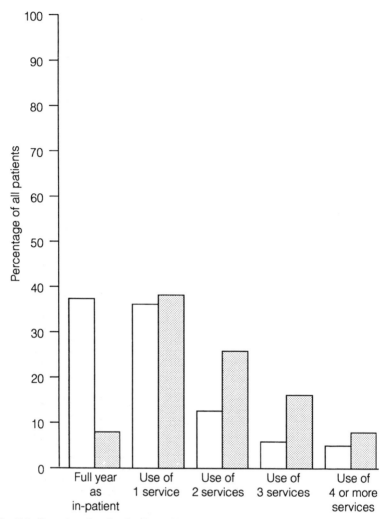

Fig. 12.2. Comparison of number of services used in 1974 (☐) and in 1985 (▨) by patients on the register

An earlier study (Hassall & Rose, 1988) has shown that, for the elderly, it would be of value for existing registers to increase information gathered to include additional local-authority services such as home helps, and residence in sheltered accommodation. Without this information, there is a danger that the substantial support received from such services by elderly people in psychiatric care is underestimated and that their ability to survive in the community is attributed only to care provided by the National Health Service.

The information given above illustrates some of the data which can be extracted from a case register, which it is not possible to obtain from other records. Most of the newly implemented patient-recording systems do not

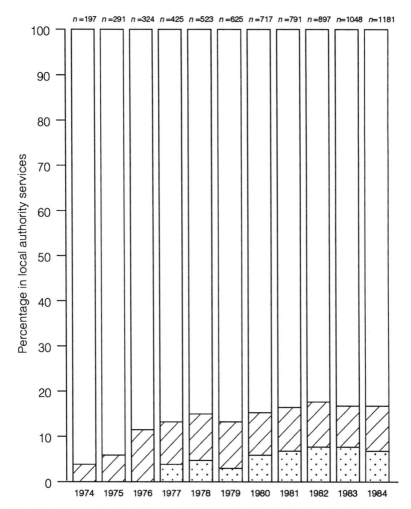

Fig. 12.3. Patients registered from 1 January 1974 – proportion in local-authority services (social work and day centre) each year (□ , no social work or day care; ▨ , social work or day care with other services; ⊡ social work or day care only)

include such comprehensive data nor, for the most part, are they equipped to store extensive longitudinal histories of patient care. While it is not suggested that case registers should be maintained in every district, they are a valuable and unique source of information.

Reference

HASSALL, C. & ROSE, S. (1989) Powick Hospital 1978–86. A case register study. In *Contributions to Health Service Planning and Research* (ed. J. K. Wing). London: Gaskell.

13 The needs and burdens of the elderly mentally ill

IAN F. BROCKINGTON, WENDY MORRIS and ERIC JONES

The Department of Health and Social Security (DHSS) commissioned a study of the problem of the elderly mentally ill in the Worcester Development Project, and we conducted a survey of subjects over 75 years of age. The original purpose was to find out how well the Worcester Development Project dealt with the problem of the elderly, although in the course of our study, we diverged from that original intention. Our objectives were to diagnose mental illness, both organic and functional, to identify the needs imposed by it, to determine on whom the burden fell, and to find out to what extent the needs were being met. From the original sample of 759 subjects, we excluded 38 who had died before it was drawn and one who was under the age of 75, leaving 720 for interview. Sixteen were lost altogether, 69 died between sampling and approach, and 210 refused the interview; every attempt was made to obtain information on those who had died or refused interview. In the end, we interviewed 413 and had some information on 642: this is a 3% sample of the 21 000 persons on the over-75 register in the Worcester Development Project. We checked the validity of the sampling frame by studying 100 consecutive death certificates, and found that eight of those who died were not on the register of those aged over 75.

We used a screening interview which was designed to cover mental and physical health, social support, and the circumstances of daily living. The data were recorded in narrative and diagnoses made polydiagnostically, using multiple raters. We studied the validity of the primary interview in a series of 56 subjects, who also had psychiatric interviews using the Geriatric Mental State Interview (Copeland et al, 1976). The reliability, concordance with consensus diagnoses, sensitivity, and specificity of the primary interview diagnoses were high for organic mental illness, but lower for functional illness (Jones et al, 1988). We therefore narrowed the definition of functional mental illness, deciding that subjective and objective evidence of anxiety or depression must be present, lasting for at least a month, and the subject must have sought treatment, had a wish to die, or had a functional deficit resulting from those symptoms. This proved to be a fairly strict definition, but not

TABLE 13.1
Severe forgetfulness by sex and age range[1]

	75–79	80–84	85–89	90–94	95–99	Total
			Age range: years			
Women						
No. in age group	98	103	53	16	5	275
No. of sufferers	12	9	3	6[2]	1	31
% of age range	12	9	6	33		11
Men						
No. in age range	71	50	11	5	1	138
No. of sufferers	5	2	2	–	–	9
% of age range	7	4	12			7

1. Interviewed sample only.
2. Includes two patients with intermittent confusion. If they are excluded, frequency in age group 90–99 is 24%.

inappropriately so, because patients who meet those criteria do require treatment. Of the indices we measured, the most important was the sensitivity of the primary interview, because that initiated the diagnostic process. This sensitivity proved to be high, if two research workers reviewed the data in the interview.

We considered the problem of *severe forgetfulness*. This was defined by evidence of a failure to learn on memory testing and a small number of errors on the cognitive testing, without any functional deficit due to brain failure. This was very common, being present in 10% of the sample interviewed (Table 13.1). Furthermore, we could detect minor but definite degrees of memory failure in a considerably larger number – perhaps 25–30% of those aged over 75. When we studied the age and sex distribution of this phenomenon, it was found to be more common in women; indeed 33% of women of extreme age (90 or above) had severe forgetfulness.

We found 67 subjects with *dementia*. Many had died between sampling and approach, and it seems important in this kind of research to conduct a 'rolling survey', because of the high death rate among demented people. The age distribution of those with dementia was interesting (Table 13.2). In males between 75 and 80 it was 7%, falling to 5% between 80 and 84, rising slightly to 9% in those aged over 85. In women, the figure was 5% for those aged 75–79, 8% in those aged 80–84, after which it jumped to 25% in the age group 85–89, and 40% between 95 and 99. Thus, there appeared to be a marked difference between men and women, which does not seem to be widely recognised. Furthermore, the idea that dementia is a problem which looms at the age of 65, or even 75, does not seem accurate; it is essentially a problem of the over-85s, especially in women. However, it should be borne in mind that the main purpose of this research was not to carry out an epidemiological survey and that it was a prevalence study; it is possible that the enormous increase in prevalence in women is at least partly due

TABLE 13.2

Senile dementia (SD) by sex, age range and sample size

| | Age range: years | | | | | | | | | | | |
| | 75–79 | | 80–84 | | 85–89 | | 90–94 | | 95–99 | | Total | |
	No. of sufferers	No. in sample	No. of sufferers	No. in sample	No. of sufferers	No. in sample	No. of sufferers	No. in sample	No. of sufferers	No. in sample	No. of sufferers	No. in sample
Women												
Interviewed	3	99	6	103	13	53	7	16	2	5	31	276[1]
Refused	1	41	2	34	1	18	1	10	–	1	5	104[2]
Died	3	8	4	12	7	14	1	5	2	4	17	43
Totals	7	148	12	149	21	85	9	31	4	10	53	423
% of age range	5		8		25		29		40		13	
Men												
Interviewed	1	73	3	50	–	11	1	5	–	1	5	140[1]
Refused	3	22	–	23	2	7	–	1	–	–	5	53[2]
Died	3	12	1	5	–	5	–	2	–	2	4	26
Totals	7	107	4	78	2	23	1	8	–	3	14	219
% of age range	7		5		9		9				6	

1. Sample size includes two proxy interviews and one full account by letter.
2. Sample size includes four who were too ill to be interviewed.

to their greater physical survival when demented. If dementia and severe forgetfulness are combined, then 80% of women in extreme old age had mental impairment.

How are these people supported and cared for? There were 78 subjects in the whole sample in residential care: 41 in private residential care, 10 in voluntary-aided care, 21 in Part-III (local-authority social-services) accommodation, two in a geriatric ward, and only four in a psychiatric ward. If subjects with dementia are considered, 40 out of 67 were in residential care: 17 of those were in private nursing homes, seven in private rest homes, only one in a voluntary-aided home, ten in Part-III accommodation, two in a geriatric ward, and three in a psychiatric ward. We found no evidence that the more severe cases were in hospital, rather than in social-services homes or private homes; in fact, the opposite was true. It was possible to determine which patients had severe physical disorder as well as dementia, and we found that 17 of 32 people in private homes and only 7 of 23 in the social-services home or the hospitals had this combination. In other words, it appeared that the more severely ill people were in private homes. We also noted that there were five people with extreme incapacity – three of whom were in private homes, one in a social-services home, and one in a hospital. The costs of the private nursing homes was £125–250 per week. Part-III accommodation cost £161 per week, which is quite moderate in comparison, but it was difficult to obtain comparable data for hospitals. The Lucy Baldwin Unit in Kidderminster cost £350 per week, which is much higher than the private homes, but the figure for the Elgar Unit appeared to be lower. The estimated cost of private residential care in Worcester and Kidderminster health districts is £10 million a year, whilst the total budgets of the National Health Service mental health units are somewhat higher than that. On the same basis, the nationwide cost would be about £1 billion for private residential care. Before completing this tally of those in residential care, it should be mentioned that six of the subjects with dementia were taken into the homes of their sons or daughters, and two into the homes of nieces, while one remained in her own home, nursed by a rota of resident daughters who came in for a fortnight at a time. Thus, families provided some of the 'residential care'.

It seemed clear that the majority of people who were taken into residential care had never had any assessment by psychiatrists or by social workers. This could be a serious omission, because some may have had treatable disorders. The lack of assessment means that there is no opportunity to try to keep people in their own homes and to support them there. But to assess all these elderly people with brain failure would require much more resources.

Of the demented subjects who were not in residential care, six were living alone, some of them having physical illness as well; one of them was in day care for two days a week. Two were largely supported by wardens, and another two had much support from home helps. Fifteen other subjects were living out of residential care, with family members or with their spouses;

some of them had a major physical illness as well as dementia. Of these 15 living with families or their spouse, two were in day-hospital care for five days a week and one was in day-hospital care for two days a week, so that there was an underprovision of day care. Two of them had daily visits from a nurse, one had twice-weekly visits and one had once-weekly visits; there appeared to be unmet need in eight subjects.

Turning to functional mental illness, it was surprising how little was found. Almost all the definitions of depression used in modern surveys report illnesses lasting at least *two* weeks; we defined ours as lasting at least a month, so that our definition was more stringent. The effect of differences in definition was shown by our polydiagnostic study in Kidderminster, where 141 people were interviewed. Twenty-seven met some criteria for depression or functional mental illness and the same number scored 5 on the General Health Questionnaire (GHQ; Goldberg, 1972) but only 14 met Research Diagnostic Criteria (RDC; Spitzer *et al*, 1978) for episodic minor depression or anxiety, and when two psychiatrists studied the data and made consensus diagnoses using our strict criteria, there were only five definite 'cases'. It was remarkable what a good state of morale most elderly people had, and how happy they were, how well adjusted, and what a very small number were severely depressed. Even so, it was disturbing that well over half of those who *were* depressed were not in treatment, perhaps because elderly depressed people do not refer themselves for treatment.

Who is supporting the elderly? We counted the number of visits (made at least once a week) by different people – 1194 visits to 366 subjects not in residential care (Table 13.3). On average, two visits per week were made by family members and two-thirds of all visits were made by them. The average number of visits was low if a person had already been taken into the home of a relative, and it was relatively low for fit subjects. The highest number of visits (over three a week) was made to those who were housebound by physical illness. Thus, the response of the families can rise by 50%, especially if an elderly relative has severe physical illness.

TABLE 13.3
Number of visits made to elderly people not in residential care

	All interviewed at home (n = 1194)	All housebound	All living alone	All demented	Demented living alone
No. of subjects	366	91	181	13	4
Visits by family members	798	258	469	33	12
average number/week	2.18	2.87	2.59	2.54	3.00
Visits by friends and voluntary agencies	161	35	147	2	1
Paid support	59	32	37	2	0
Statutory support	176	88	115	19	12

Another important source of support is neighbours and friends: we found that the amount of support offered by them was about the same as the statutory support – a total of about 150 visits per week in all. On the other hand, the private sector, which is making such a major contribution to residential care, makes only a very small contribution to domiciliary care.

For statutory care, one first has to consider wardens, who are an important source of support for the elderly; they are financed partly by social services and partly by housing organisations. We found that just over one-fifth of all subjects were in warden-assisted accommodation, and to some extent this was given preferentially to the mentally ill (54%); however, there was only one demented person on our list who was in warden-assisted accommodation. Apart from wardens, the main source of statutory help was the home helps, provided by social services. Community psychiatric nurses and social workers do not appear on the list of regular visitors, but that is because their visits were not usually as often as once a week, and only visits once a week or more were included under the heading of 'close support'.

For home helps and other statutory helpers, the average was one half of a visit per week for the whole survey population, but special efforts were made by them for the mentally ill; subjects with dementia were at the top of the list, with an average of three visits a week, so that this is a form of support which is preferentially given to those with brain failure.

The overall impression is that a great deal is being done to help the aged in the Worcester Development Project area and that it is being done by a wide variety of people. Worcester and Kidderminster are well supplied with psychogeriatric services – more so than most districts. Even so, these services are seriously overstretched: they have too many people to see, and yet the psychogeriatric services are making a very small contribution to the total picture of care. There is clearly a major problem in setting up services to deal with the challenge of mental illness in the elderly.

References

COPELAND, J. R. M., KELLEHER, M. J., KELLETT, J. M., *et al* (1976) A semi-structured clinical interview for the assessment of diagnosis and mental state in the elderly: the Geriatric Mental State Schedule. *Psychological Medicine*, **6**, 439–449.

GOLDBERG, D. P. (1972) *The Detection of Psychiatric Illness by Questionnaire*. London: Oxford University Press.

JONES, E., MORRIS, W., COOPER, P., *et al* (1988) *The Needs and Burdens of the Elderly Mentally Ill*. Unpublished report to the DHSS.

SPITZER, R. L., ENDICOTT, J. & ROBINS, E. (1978) *Research Diagnostic Criteria (RDC) for a Selected Group of Functional Disorders* (3rd edn). New York: New York State Psychiatric Institute.

14 A measurement of the standards of care

CHARLES BARKER

Defining the quality of health care is a challenge. Over the years, the concept has never been ignored, and the various structures of the National Health Service (NHS) have always carried responsibilities related to 'monitoring', 'assessing' and 'evaluating' – all of these being included in the job descriptions held by managers and clinical staff alike.

Ryland & Richards (1987) describe the progress that has been made on quality measurement as 'continuous audit', and they highlight the influence that NHS reorganisations, various official reports, the input from bodies like the Health Advisory Service, and the regular inspection undertaken by academic and validatory bodies such as the General Nursing Council and the medical royal colleges have contributed. These sound, but fragmented, attempts have contributed much towards the interest now being shown in this subject generally.

My own introduction to quality assurance began in 1986, when our unit general manager forwarded to his managers a copy of a memorandum from the Secretary of the District Health Authority and Director of Health Care Services, Worcester and District Health Authority, on the subject of the registration and inspection of private nursing homes. They asked us to consider whether the long-stay wards in our units met the standards expected of private nursing homes. We had to confess, though, that we could not answer the question. Although we felt that the service in the long-stay areas was acceptable and could compare favourably with the private sector, we recognised that our views were solely subjective. There was a need to explore further a means by which we could measure and then compare standards between our own district mental health services for long-stay patients and those of the private sector. If we could do this, we could then answer the question objectively. The task was delegated to me.

As a relative newcomer to the field of quality assurance, I found that there were many excellent reviews of the subject. One important piece of advice was particularly noted – the need to conduct a literature search of existing audit tools to ascertain whether or not they would meet our requirements, but I was unable to discover any that would measure and compare the services we provided with the standard expected of nursing homes in the private sector. I therefore needed to identify the demands made upon the private sector, in relation to the registration of nursing homes. To do this, copies were obtained of *Guidelines and Procedures Document for the Registration and Conduct of Nursing Homes*, produced by Worcester and District Health Authority, *Home Life: A Code of Practice for Residential Care* (DHSS report) and the *Nursing Homes and Mental Nursing Homes Regulations 1984* (H84/1346) (DHSS statutory instrument no. 1578, appendix 3). From these, I emerged with the following list of areas ('sections') which I hoped to measure:

(1) admission procedure
(2) terms and conditions
(3) general administration
(4) privacy and personal autonomy
(5) financial affairs
(6) health care
(7) dying and death
(8) physical features
(9) diet and food preparation
(10) client group
(11) disabled people
(12) mentally ill people
(13) mentally handicapped people
(14) young people
(15) elderly people
(16) drug/alcohol/solvent abuse
(17) staff
(18) responsibilities of the authority
(19) kitchens
(20) records (patients)
(21) records (staff)
(22) records (fire safety)
(23) records (maintenance of equipment)
(24) records (retention of records)
(25) records (notification/death)
(26) accident prevention
(27) control of infection
(28) linen and laundry
(29) fire prevention
(30) disposal of infected/waste material.

Having identified and selected what could be measured, I had reached the stage where an appropriate audit tool needed to be designed, to incorporate the good practices given in the three publications previously mentioned.

Section 6 (Health care)
Statement 2

Tick response

	Correct 11.1%	Correct but needs improving 5.5%	No 0%	Does not apply
Patients are not given treatment without their consent except in life-threatening circumstances and under the terms of the Mental Health Act				

Comments	Action agreed	Review date	Outcome

Auditor guidelines

Seek proof.
Check knowledge of
staff at ward level

Audit date:

Auditor's signature:

Fig. 14.1. An example of one item on the Standards of Care and Practice Audit (SCAPA) form. There are nine statements in Section 6, giving a possible total of 100% for 'Correct' and 50% for 'Correct but needs improving'

In this, each section would contain an appropriate number of relevant statements ('indicators'), each of which would carry a score percentage, according to the quality identified. It was anticipated that this would provide an overall picture of the quality of the services within the sections audited, and this was eventually achieved by the design of a score sheet. I then rewrote the advice and guidance contained in the three reference sources and produced the measurable indicators that were required within the audit sections.

The statements (indicators) carry the following score rating: a 'correct' response is awarded 100%, while a 'correct but needs improving' response receives 50%, this being the lowest level within the 'safe-practice zone' of the scale on the score sheet. The total result can be identified by a dot on the score sheet, after all the responses have been calculated for that section. At the end of this exercise, the completed audit tool contained 30 sections and an overall number of 240 statements. An example is shown in Fig. 14.1. The audit document was called *Standards of Care and Practice Audit* (SCAPA).

In order to reach conclusions on manpower requirement, I devised and piloted a 'priority for care study', based on six 'priority for care indicators', which focused on high-risk circumstances, each indicator requiring a 'yes' or 'no' response. These responses, when scored and calculated, give information on the 'phase of care' and on the staffing requirements needed to meet the demands made over the 24-hour period that is forecast.

In order to reach the calculations shown in the SCAPA document, I used the time allowances identified in the "The Report of the Nursing Workload and Quality of Care Study in 21 Wards" (North Lincolnshire Health Authority). This decision was made following a comparative study of the care requirements of both physically ill and mentally ill elderly patients.

Having produced the audit tool, I decided to use it to measure the standards of care and practice at Sheffield House, a community unit for ex-long-stay patients who had been transferred from Powick Hospital. In March 1987, I had my first meeting with the staff of Sheffield House, at which they were introduced to the audit tool I would be using, and the method by which I would be working was outlined.

As a result of this meeting the following decisions were made:

(a) the manager of the unit and his/her immediate manager would need to be present at all audit interviews
(b) other staff members would have an open invitation to attend, depending on service needs
(c) interviews would not exceed two hours
(d) comments recorded by the auditor would be discussed and action required recorded
(e) where possible, action required would be given a timescale to enable change to be accomplished within that period

(f) the audit would be treated as confidential and its contents made known only to the staff of Sheffield House, their immediate manager, and the unit general manager

(g) a record would be kept identifying the statement numbers (for reference to the problem), the recommendations made, and the timescale negotiated to achieve results.

The value of this meeting cannot be overemphasised: it allowed frank discussion, and paved the way for the commencement of the audit. Overall, this took eight hours to complete (four sessions), out of which a list of 44 recommendations were recorded. Using the audit helped to develop a sense of awareness and insight, which might otherwise have gone unrecognised; the staff wasted no time in working through the recommendations. As a result, they were able to say, quite definitely, that Sheffield House compared very favourably with the services expected of the private sector. Following this first complete pilot run, SCAPA continued to be used as a means of measuring the quality of care provided throughout the mental health unit.

As with all measurement tools, the outcome was to identify what was being provided by the service at the time of auditing. It is up to the managers and staff to move to the next stage.

I would recommend all managers to venture into this new and challenging area, since measurement tools offer insight, rather than assumptions, as to what goes on within our services.

Acknowledgements

My thanks are due to the staff of the Mental Health Unit, Worcester and District Health Authority, and to Mrs Delia E. Hudson, Founder Chairman, National Association of Quality Assurance.

Reference

RYLAND, R. & RICHARDS, F. (1987) Where the buck stops. *Senior Nurse*, **16**, 6–7.

III. Home treatment

15 A systems approach to the treatment of people with chronic mental illness

LEONARD STEIN

As the model programme, run by 'missionary staff', in the Worcester Development Project will be different from running a service for an entire geographical area, a service developed in Wisconsin, an area similar to Worcester, is described in this chapter.

State mental hospitals were developed in the United States around 1850. By the very early 1900s, they had appeared all over the country, and soon became overcrowded. Wards built for 25 patients were holding 50, 75, and even more, so that by the mid-1940s, they were essentially warehouses for human beings who had been discarded by society. There were a number of factors that later influenced the deinstitutionalisation or depopulation of those hospitals, including effective medication for psychosis and an increase in the number of mental health professionals after World War II – for instance, from about 3000 psychiatrists in 1945 to over 30 000 at present. The principle of treatment near home was discovered in World War I, forgotten, and rediscovered in World War II. Clinical research supported community care, legal actions were introduced to protect the rights of patients, and there were also economic motives, which were perhaps the most important. The first year, from the time they were built, that the population in state mental hospitals began to drop, was 1955; 1965–75 was a period of rapid depopulation, when resident patients declined from 550 000 to approximately 120 000. That is generally called 'the period of deinstitutionalisation', but the readmission rate to hospital increased dramatically at about the same time, and there were other negative consequences to depopulating hospitals. Many mentally ill patients were homeless and neglected, and began to drift into the orbit of the criminal justice system. Large numbers of patients were moved from hospitals into nursing homes, which often were worse than the hospitals they came from (transinstitutionalisation).

In our own progressive mental hospital, we had well staffed wards, with 25 patients to a ward, each of which had two psychiatrists, a psychologist, nurses and aides. We provided all the necessary requirements for stable adjustment on the ward – food, shelter, clothing, medical treatment, social activities, vocational training, and recreation. Our average length of stay was relatively short, about 21 days. We made good discharge plans, sent the person out into the community after we had stabilised their psychosis and regulated their medication. However, our patients still suffered from long-term impairments, which interfered with their ability to make a stable adjustment to community life. These long-term impairments were secondary to the negative symptoms of schizophrenia, to residual psychotic symptoms, to personality pathology, and sometimes to organic pathology. The affected patients were highly vulnerable to stress, had difficulty with interpersonal relationships, and a marked dependence on either family or institutions. They also had a deficiency in coping skills, such as budgeting, using public transport, shopping, cooking, and ordering meals in restaurants; moreover, we found that there was a poor transfer of the skills we taught in hospital after the patient left it.

Thus, the patient left hospital with good discharge plans and enough medication, but also with those long-term impairments; meanwhile, the hospital was still there with its staff, operating 24 hours a day, seven days a week. If he attended the mental health centre where he had an appointment some two weeks hence, they would see him, but if he did not, they would not look for him. All the other necessities of life – housing, socialisation, recreation, finance – were available, but administered by different agencies, and patients did not have staff available 24 hours a day to help them negotiate with a complicated bureaucratic system. The result was that within a relatively short time, they were generally readmitted to the hospital because medication lapsed, money ran out, or they spent their time isolated in their rooms with no one ensuring that they had some human contact. In a relatively short time, they became psychotic again and came back to hospital.

Those were the kinds of things that Dr Mary Ann Test, research clinical psychologist, and I found when we went out into the community. Patients returned for 'non-psychiatric' reasons, such as running out of money or getting evicted. We came to the conclusion that we needed to change this 'non-system' of 'care', which had a variety of different services operating independently, and change it into a system of care where services are integrated and co-ordinated. In the 'non-system', if patients get lost, nobody feels obliged to look for them; non-systems of care fail both the patients and the professionals working in them. So we moved a psychiatrist, a psychologist, a social worker, five nurses, nine aides, a ward clerk, and a ward secretary out of the hospital into an old house in downtown Madison, Wisconsin. Those staff were to work with patients coming to the hospital for admission, but instead of doing so *in* the hospital, they would work with them in the community. We set up a research design (Stein & Test, 1980): patients coming to the hospital for admission would be assigned to either the experimental programme or the control programme, and we would collect data at baseline and every four months. Some of the patients we received into the study were brought in handcuffs by the police, were brought by their families, or were transferred from psychiatric units of general hospitals because they 'could not be managed there' or 'needed further care' (which generally meant that their insurance had run out!). Thus we took anyone provided that they were resident in the county in which our hospital was located, were between the ages of 18 and 62, and had any diagnosis other than primary alcoholism or severe organic brain disease. There were 65 patients in each group: they were relatively young, 'revolving-door' patients, of whom at least 50% had schizophrenia, and 73% were single, separated, or divorced. They had already spent on average 14½ months in hospital, divided over five prior admissions, so that this would have been about their sixth admission. We collected information about where they were living, how much time they spent in institutions, their employment, leisure activities, social relationships, the quality of the environment they were living in, how satisfied they were with their lives, a measure of their self-esteem, and an assessment of their symptoms.

The control patients were admitted to the hospital as usual and treated for the usual amount of time (an average of 21 days). Discharge plans were made and they were sent out to the usual kinds of community services available in the United States. This included a mental health centre which primarily did psychotherapy with relatively healthy people, but had some services for mentally ill people including medication, evaluation and monitoring, and some activities in the evenings and during the day. These services, though, were only given if the patient showed up; if not, people shrugged their shoulders and said "isn't it too bad that this patient isn't motivated to come in and get treatment."

The experimental group were looked after by the community team, who worked in an old house in downtown Madison, which was used not as a place to treat patients or where patients slept, but where staff made their plans and worked *out of* (not a place they worked *in*). They operated two shifts a day, seven days a week; the first would arrive at 7.00 a.m. and the second at 2.30 p.m., with an hour overlap between shifts; the evening shift would return at 10.30 p.m. One of the professionals remained on call during the night, so that we had cover 24 hours a day, seven days a week. We used two sets of principles – working with patients and working with the community. We discovered that just as there are interventions to help patients live in the community, there are also interventions which will help the community learn to live with patients.

The manner of working

Let us consider that house at 7 a.m., where the morning shift has gathered to work. They had 65 patients to care for, each of whom was listed on a card index, just as in hospital. The morning shift would read every card, taking perhaps 45 minutes for all 65 patients, and the discussion would be something like the following:

> "Joe Brown: Joe's not having any trouble. Jane Smith: Jane is having trouble with her landlord. Somebody's got to go out there today, work with the landlord and Jane, take care of that problem; who's going to do that?" Somebody would volunteer or somebody would be chosen. They go through the next few people. No problems. Then they get to Phil Brown. "Phil is having problems with his family. Somebody's got to go out there today and work that out . . . Joe Smith is running out of money. We've got to go to the welfare office and get him some and then we have to set up a budgeting scheme for him where we'll dish out his money on a weekly basis, or sometimes even on a daily basis, so that that doesn't happen again, until he learns better how to care for his money". Then they come to William Smith, and people look at each other, puzzled. "What's happening to William Smith?" Since we don't know what's happening to William Smith, somebody goes out to find him, have coffee with him, and find out what's going on.

By 8.00 a.m. there is only the secretary left at the telephone. The rest of the staff is carrying out the assignments. They return at 2.30 p.m., when there is a meeting between the morning and afternoon shifts; the morning shift report and go through the card index once again. Assignments are made for the evening shift. They go out, return at 10.30 p.m., write in the logbook what the morning shift needs to know, and the morning shift arrives next morning. Essentially, they do whatever is necessary to ensure that the patients make a stable adjustment to life, and are helped with their problems. We did not regard any matters of concern as outside our sphere.

Results of the trial

There was essentially no increased cost in treating the patients in the community, compared with in the hospital (Weisbrod *et al*, 1980; Stein, 1987). This study has now been replicated several times, mostly again with a decrease in cost. We studied the burden on families and the community, and found that there was no increase in the burden on the family or the community; in a few of our measures, there was actually a decrease in the burden (Test & Stein, 1980).

Clinically, there was a tremendous difference between the experimental and control groups. In the first year, 57 of the 65 control patients were admitted to hospital, for an average of 36 days per patient. The readmission rate was very high – 60% – so the control patients continued to revolve in and out of hospital.

However, only 12 of the 65 experimental patients were admitted to hospital, for a mean of 11 days per patient. But if hospital stay was the only thing that had been measured, that would not be doing very much. However, a measure of independent living showed that the experimental group did significantly better than the control group. A measure of employment was also significantly better for the experimental group, but there was no difference in leisure activities. Social relationships were significantly better in the experimental group. The quality of the environment was good for both groups. The experimental group experienced and reported a higher satisfaction with life, the longer the experiment went on. There was a tremendous difference in symptoms between the two groups, with much less morbidity in the experimental group.

The important question then is, what happened after we stopped? We collected data for a further 14 months. We found that the gains we had made began to be lost, so that by the end of the study, there was a definite deterioration, measured in terms of hospital stay, employment, social relationships, etc. This might appear to be a very disappointing finding, but we came to the conclusion that it was the most important finding of the entire study. All of our care programmes in the United States, at this time, whether hospital or community, were previously time limited, established to prepare patients to live in the community. We had day-treatment programmes lasting three months or six months, after which they were no longer thought to need them. We had quarter-way houses and half-way houses, after which patients were assumed no longer to need that kind of help. The very important principle that we came to after this study was that there must be no arbitrary time limits for services to patients: they must be allowed to move at their own pace. Patients can certainly move from more intensive to less intensive services, but you cannot predict when this should be.

The system developed

We took what we learned in this study and translated it to change an entire community, so that it would adhere to these principles of care. We felt very strongly that mental health centres in the United States had their priorities turned upside down: they were spending most of their time, energy, and resources working with people who were not seriously ill. No doubt they were helping those people, but the consequences of not getting their help would not have been disastrous. We thought that we needed to spend most of our resources and energy working with the very seriously ill, where the consequences of not getting appropriate support and care are indeed disastrous, with relapse into psychosis, disruption of life, disruption of their families, and relocation back into a hospital. Our system was not achieved easily or quickly, but now, some 14 years later, it is recognised as a model for how a community can provide services to the seriously and persistently mentally ill.

In Wisconsin, the state has decentralised its power to the county, a local-government entity, which is the central authority, responsible for planning and operationalising the service. Dane County is very much like Worcestershire, being an attractive rural area. The largest city is Madison with a population of 180 000; the total population in the county is 340 000, so that outside Madison there are small towns and farms. The county is approximately 50 miles by 50 miles, square in shape. The central authority is a county mental health board that plans and organises the services; it has control over the mental health budget. There is no separate budget for hospital or community services; all the money is controlled by the central authority, which pays for whatever services it uses, but no more. There must be a fixed point of responsibility for every patient in the system.

We identified about 1500 people with severe and persistent mental illness, and we know the name of every one of them and the person in our system who is responsible for that individual. Those details are held in our computer. We have three services that take responsibility for these 1500 patients, depending on the intensity of care that a patient needs, and his/her willingness to attend for services. If a patient is willing to meet appointments, some kind of peripatetic service will not be needed. But there are many patients who are not willing to do so, and therefore you need a service that is organised so that it can go out and provide services where the patient is. Medication compliance is another factor. Then there is the need for structured daily activity. Some patients have their own network and do not require services to provide activities for them, but others would be sitting alone in their rooms, if activities were not provided for them. There are differences in the ability of patients to monitor themselves. Some patients, when they become symptomatic, know they are getting ill again and seek help before their next appointment. Other patients think that someone is after them, and they hide; so very different responses are needed for those kinds of patients.

We have a mobile community treatment team, a service concerned with the needs of the subgroup of patients that are the most difficult to treat – those that are generally unwilling to attend clinics, with poor medication compliance, poor self-monitoring, frequent crises, etc. This service operates in the same way as the one that I described in the experiment, with two shifts a day, seven days a week, with 20 patients per staff member – it should be no more than 10 per staff member, but we are a poor county. This service looks after about 200 of the most difficult patients. Our day-treatment service works on the model of the New York Foundation House Clubhouse. It is progressive, vocationally orientated and helps patients to uphold their own rights. This service works with an intermediate group of patients, and has a lower staff : patient ratio than the mobile team. The third service is our out-patient clinic; it works with a more stable group of seriously ill patients, who are willing to attend, who know they are ill, and who are willing to take their medicine. Here, much higher numbers of patients per staff member can be accepted.

All three services conceptualise their job as not just monitoring medication or being interested in the patient's psychological symptoms. They are also interested in the patient's living situation, finances, social activities, etc., all of which influence the patient's psychological well-being. All services can see patients in their homes if necessary.

Cutting across all three services is our crisis stabilisation and resolution service. This operates 24 hours a day, seven days a week. Most crisis units in the United States are evaluation and disposition units: they see people and they evaluate them, to decide where they should go. In many of our cities, crisis units operate out of emergency rooms of hospitals and act as funnels into the hospital. Since our emergency unit is given the task of resolving the crisis, they not only see the person once, but will do so several times a day if necessary. They will carry that person for weeks on end, if needed, until the crisis is stabilised. If the person needs continuing care, he/she is moved into one of the other three services. The unit takes care of new people coming into the system in crisis, or it works with the other services if there is a crisis and another service needs help in managing it. For example, the day-treatment unit does not operate at night, so if the unit needs some help after 9 p.m., the crisis unit will do it. Our out-patient clinic does not operate at weekends, and if a patient needs visiting at the weekend, the crisis unit will do it. Thus, the services are integrated and work together to provide round-the-clock care for all patients.

The managers or leaders of each service meet every week to talk about transferring patients from one service to another, or about new patients. Transfers are made by handing the patient over from one staff member to another, usually with a meeting between the two staff members and the patient. Transfers from one service to another may be done gradually, over as long as a year. With this population, it is best to think not in terms of months or even one or two years, but rather in terms of five years and ten years. When you work with patients and their families over many years, this is tremendously satisfying.

We have a policy that no one is admitted to hospital unless the crisis team authorises it. If somebody is admitted the team that manages the patient meets the in-patient team on the first day of that admission. As a result, our hospital days have dropped dramatically in Dane County. Overall, the quality of life for our patients is exceedingly good: we have people living in very good housing, and they are not merely watching television all day. The money that we are able to spend on community services is only there because we save it on in-patient services. The national average in the United States is to spend 70% of funding on in-patient services and 30% on out-patient services. In Dane County, we spend 85% on out-patient community services, and only 15% on in-patient services. We receive less money than the national average and the only reason we can run such a good service is because we are able to distribute our resources well.

If deinstitutionalisation is defined correctly (i.e. as a reduction of the use of the hospital and the concomitant development of comprehensive community services), it has been successful everywhere it has been attempted.

Homelessness, mentally ill people in gaol, and high readmission rates occur where hospitals have been depopulated without developing services in the community. It appears that the Worcester Development Project has defined deinstitutionalisation correctly, and thus comprehensive community services are available for patients transferred from hospital into the community.

References

STEIN, L. I. (1987) Funding a system of care for schizophrenia. *Psychiatric Annals*, **17**, 592–598.
—— & TEST, M. A. (1980) Alternative to mental hospital treatment – I. Conceptual model, treatment program, and clinical evaluation. *Archives of General Psychiatry*, **37**, 392–397.
TEST, M. A. & STEIN, L. I. (1980) Alternative to mental hospital treatment – III. Social cost. *Archives of General Psychiatry*, **37**, 409–412.
WEISBROD, B., TEST, M. A. & STEIN, L. I. (1980) Alternative to mental hospital treatment – II. Economic benefit–cost analysis. *Archives of General Psychiatry*, **37**, 400–405.

16 Home treatment in New South Wales

JOHN HOULT

My theme is that the quality of care and the quality of life for the mentally ill can be improved. Demonstration research projects have proved this; they are able to influence government policy, and their principles of care can be applied in the real world. However, perseverance is needed to make it happen, and we have to get the structures and the organisation of the services right.

New South Wales is the most highly populated of the six states and two territories which form the Commonwealth of Australia. It has 5.5 million inhabitants, of whom 3.3 million live in Sydney, the state capital. Before and during the 1950s, there was in New South Wales virtually only one type of service for the severely mentally ill, as there was everywhere else – the mental hospitals – and they were understaffed, overcrowded, squalid, and neglected. In 1960, there was a Royal Commission in Sydney into allegations of cruelty and neglect at one of the mental hospitals. Its damning report prompted the state government to make major changes: money was poured into the mental hospitals, wards were refurbished, staff levels were improved and morale soared. There was a change in how patients were dealt with: many from the long-stay wards were placed in nursing homes or boarding houses, and those newly admitted stayed only a few weeks. It was less easy for the new patients to become 'long stay', and to replace those in the long-stay wards who had left. However, follow-up care was provided only by a few domiciliary nurses from the mental hospitals, and by doctors conducting out-patient clinics at the mental hospitals for those patients who were compliant enough to travel the long distances from their homes, but many did not comply and were lost to follow-up. Moreover, overcrowding remained a problem throughout the 1960s. Community mental health services continued to be puny until 1973, when the commonwealth government gave very large financial grants to the state governments to set up community services. There was a sudden large expansion in them in New South Wales, but sadly, the US experience was repeated, the staff quickly found a new clientele – doing psychotherapy with the worried well, or unspecified 'primary prevention', which took priority over the care and rehabilitation of the severely mentally ill, who continued to be a neglected group in the 1970s.

At about this time, the link between the mental hospitals and community mental health centres was severed, and the centres no longer became the outreach component of the hospitals, but quite independent of them, so that liaison and co-ordination suffered. By 1975, concern was being expressed that sufficient action was not being taken to care for chronic patients who had been discharged into the community. But nothing happened, and the numbers in the mental hospitals continued to drop.

In the early 1980s, the worsening economic climate for both common-wealth and state governments, combined with the removal of taxation advantages available to private landlords, resulted in a severe shortage of housing in New South Wales. The numbers of homeless people increased dramatically and among them, of course, were the mentally ill, who became one of the main victims of this housing crisis. Increasingly, they lost out in the battle for scarce low-cost housing, and ended up on the streets. A survey of Sydney's largest shelter for the homeless in 1988 showed that 25% of the occupants had schizophrenia. Few of these schizophrenic patients had been long-stay patients in mental hospitals: only 8% had ever spent more than one year continuously in hospital. They were the new patients who stay in hospital for a short time, get better and leave, have multiple admissions, and eventually lose their connections with their family and their social networks, so that they end up isolated and in these shelters. The former long-stay patients do not seem to go to the shelters.

By 1985, the population of New South Wales had increased by one-third in 20 years, but the number of residents with mental illness in mental hospitals had fallen from 9000 in 1965 to 2100. The number of people with schizophrenia had fallen from 4700 to 1300. The majority of the mentally ill were no longer in hospitals. The admission rate, as elsewhere, had risen, although it peaked in 1980 at 27 000 and has fallen each year since then. However, while the patients have gone from the hospitals, the staff there have increased, from 5000 to over 7000! Hospitals continue to consume 80–85% of the mental health budget.

Although Sydney is a city ten times the size of Madison, Wisconsin, the programme that Stein and Test had been reporting (1978, 1980) seemed to have the necessary ingredients to make it a model of service delivery suitable for us. We decided to replicate this study in Sydney to test its applicability. However, funding was not easy to obtain, and so we had to make do with only half the number of staff used in Madison.

Our study (Hoult *et al*, 1983; Hoult, 1986) commenced in 1979. Patients who presented voluntarily or involuntarily for admission to a mental hospital were randomly allocated to experimental or control groups. The 60 experimental subjects were not admitted, if this could be avoided, but were taken back to the community and treated by a multidisciplinary team, consisting of seven staff plus one psychiatrist. The 60 control subjects were dealt with in the usual way – almost all of them were admitted to hospital for an average of about three weeks and then they were referred to one of the six community mental health centres in the catchment area for follow-up. The team treating the experimental patients worked two shifts a day, from 8 a.m. to 11 p.m., seven days a week, and one person was on call during the remaining hours. Almost all of the team's work was done in the home and in the community, not in the office. Experimental subjects who needed admission to the mental hospital remained under the care of the team psychiatrist.

After 12 months, our results (Hoult, 1986) were similar to those of Stein & Test: 60% of the experimental group were not admitted to hospital, compared with 4% of the control group, and 32% of the experimental subjects had one admission, compared with 45% of the controls. There was also a very significant difference between the groups in the lengths of stay. Most of our experimental group who were admitted stayed less than one week; only one person stayed 16 weeks or more, and that included readmissions.

The Present State Examination (PSE; Wing *et al*, 1974) was used to assess the patient's symptoms, and the experimental subjects had significantly fewer symptoms than the control group. Social adjustment did not show significant differences, although the trend on all the items was in favour of the experimental group. We asked our patients what they preferred, and they said they were very pleased not to have gone to hospital, thought they had good treatment, and would prefer to have the same again, if necessary.

To our surprise, the relatives also were very pleased and grateful that the patient had not been admitted: in spite of having the patient at home, they said they preferred it. Only a couple of relatives were unhappy: one of the experimental group was fairly upset and angry, and a couple had mixed feelings about the community policy. A typical comment was, ''I like the idea that help can be reached at any time, day or night. I feel I'm sharing the load. Mental hospital terrifies him, and now he knows he won't be admitted, he's not afraid when he's in need of treatment, so he gets treated quicker and doesn't have such a severe relapse.''

Community treatment did not result in more legal offences or police contacts and only one person, a control patient, died during the 12 months of research. A survey of all the patients in the study, three and a half years after completion, revealed that seven patients in the control group were dead. Three had definitely committed suicide, and two had drowned, both possibly suicides; two died from natural causes. No subjects in the experimental group had died at that time.

During the 12-month study period, the average treatment cost (public and private, direct and indirect), compiled by health economists at the University of New South Wales, for each patient in the experimental group was estimated at $4500, and for each control patient, $5700. Thus, the standard hospital care and after-care cost 26% more than community treatment.

The cost of treatment in the mental hospital alone for the control patients closely approximated the total cost incurred by the community-treatment group.

We included dangerous, suicidal, and acutely psychotic patients in the study. We concluded that it is feasible to treat most psychiatric patients in the community, as an alternative to hospital care, without merely transferring the burden to the community. It is preferred by patients and relatives, and can result in a better clinical outcome for less cost.

From our experience and that of others, the following principles of care seem to be important. Firstly, help needs to be intensive at the beginning: we spent a lot of time with people when they first presented. For example, I spoke to acute psychotic persons, I would think that I would not be able to treat them at home, and that I would have to admit them to hospital. But after an hour or so of talking, there was a rational part of that person that one could engage in dialogue; we kept talking, and as we did so, a solution presented itself – a way of dealing with that person at home. After another hour or so the patient and I would be in agreement, and we could make a contract about what would happen for the next few days, and that person would be taken home. Once there, we would over-visit for the first few days to reassure everyone of our availability. That time in the beginning was very important, both for the patient and for the relatives: it was a golden opportunity to form a relationship with both.

The second principle is that we actively involved both the patient and the relatives in planning; we would ask them what they thought were the possibilities and discuss various possibilities with them, to help them to realise that they were not to be passive recipients of care. They had their part to play and when they made suggestions, we would take notice of these.

Thirdly, there was consistent care by one team. While each patient would have an individual key worker, both patients and relatives accepted that there would be a team looking after them, that their key worker could not be there all the time, but that there was a personal case manager who accepted responsibility for ensuring that the patient's needs were met and for co-ordinating with other agencies. When that person could not be there, other members of the team would have to take over. The patients and relatives accepted this and related quite well to the team as a whole.

There was a preparedness to go out to the patients and the relatives assertively, but without being unnecessarily intrusive – an active rather than a passive response. Instead of waiting for things to go wrong, we would be in contact with them, and could observe relapse. If people missed appointments, we would go out and chase them up. People sometimes complain about that being unduly intrusive, but patients did not find it so, and they appreciated the attention.

We also provided help with practical problems of living *in vivo*, so that the problems of transfer of learning do not occur. In summary, this was a service that was easily accessible, responsive, which went out to the patients, and was available 24 hours a day. It gave the patients and the relatives a feeling of security, and early intervention could prevent relapse. It was an extensive, ongoing service, not a time-limited one. There are crisis services that have been criticised because they quickly settle the crisis and then leave; services of this kind bring the crisis component into disfavour. We must provide ongoing care.

After our project finished, the New South Wales government held another inquiry into services for the mentally ill. The report recommended that adequately staffed, community-based services should be set up across the state on the Madison model, and that top priority should be given to the severely mentally ill. Our research was acknowledged as being important in persuading the committee. However, the report aroused resentment through its proposals for funding the new services: 'seeding' money was to be used to set up the first of the new services, which would then reduce bed occupancy in the mental hospitals. Closures would then occur and the money so saved was to be used to establish further community-based services, which would enable further closures to occur, and so on. There was uproar, strikes, and staff refusing to allow patients to be placed out of hospital.

After a considerable delay, in mid-1984, the state government pressed ahead with implementation, which continued up until 1988. At that time, the government lost power to the Liberal Party, which allied itself with the unions against the programme.

Most community mental health staff probably now acknowledge the severely mentally ill to be their top priority, which is an important achievement. We now have ten crisis teams, serving approximately one-third of the major metropolitan centres in New South Wales; in country areas, there are teams serving a similar but less intensive function. Many of the components of care for the chronically mentally ill have been put in place. Recently, we have started a number of mobile community-treatment teams, two of which seem to be functioning well. We are making an effort to keep the staff : patient ratio low for them, and there is evidence that they are making an impact. In 1988, some 30 new staff commenced work in an inner-city area, specifically targeting their efforts on the homeless mentally ill, and reports from the shelter managers indicate that this has made an enormous difference to the situation. The mentally ill people are no longer causing problems there. Clinics are held on most days in the shelters, and there is a crisis team, readily available to visit the shelters. There is still a housing problem which needs attention, but the mentally ill are no longer neglected in the shelters. On the other hand, it cannot be denied that development across the state has been patchy, and a number of health areas have still received no new services.

How effective has this all been? Unfortunately, research was not incorporated into the new programme; just before it commenced, almost all health services research staff were removed from the Health Department by the minister. However, two small studies have been done. In the first

(Andrews *et al*, 1990), all the long-stay patients placed out of the hospital under the programme (205) were assessed. All of them were traced: not one of them was or had been homeless and none had been in gaol. They mostly co-operated with treatment and were taking their medication. Three had committed suicide – a rather high number – but of those whom we interviewed, 78% said they preferred their community treatment to the hospital, while 7% said they preferred hospital, because everything was done for them there.

The second study was of one of the ten crisis services now running in New South Wales. This service began operating in June 1986 in a middle-class area; it made a big impact on the number of admissions to the mental hospital that it served. These fell by half, from an average of 180 per annum to 95 per annum, for a catchment population of 100 000. Bed usage recorded a similar drop, and the area uses only about 4 beds in the admissions ward.

We asked the relatives how they felt about the crisis service, and 80% said they felt the patient was helped by the team. They thought that the care and treatment the patient had received from the team was better than the previous treatment. Those who work in these new crisis teams (and the new day programmes also) hear regularly from relatives how much they appreciate the ready access to help, the provision of places for patients to go, the much better ongoing care. Patients say they appreciate that they do not have to go to hospital for help. Relatives and voluntary organisations express their appreciation when new services are set up in an area, and say things are much better there. We are also noticing a phenomenon which happened in Madison; namely, that we now have relatives who say that when they have moved home, they ensure they go to an area where these new services are available.

We think that the principles of care established in demonstration projects can be transferred to ongoing services and that staff 'burn-out' is not a major problem. In fact, this is more likely to occur where there are problems with administration or bickering amongst staff. Three of the staff from the original project are still working in this way, after ten years. All of the original team regard it as the best way of working.

What is the purpose of hospital care? Hospital is a place where people go for asylum, until the treatment works and until their behaviour settles and they can be tolerated again in the community. All our treatments work outside hospital, just as well as inside. A few patients need to go to hospital for electroconvulsive therapy. Apart from that, they are there only for asylum.

The next question is what is meant by community psychiatry? It has been referred to disparagingly as people going around New York streets handing out pills and sandwiches to the homeless mentally ill. Given the impossible committal laws in New York, where treatment cannot be compelled even when patients are lying unconscious in the snow, then that is a reasonable response. Community psychiatry goes out to patients where they are.

Much of what is called community psychiatry is really not community psychiatry. It is traditional hospital psychiatry without a mental hospital: the centre of the service is still the hospital. That is where all the action is for the consultants, where they spend the majority of their time, and where the patients have to come for their follow-up. The focus is still on the acute episode, dealt with in the hospital, which for most patients will be a relapse, a failure of ongoing care. In hospital, the important activities are making the diagnosis and titrating the medication correctly. These are worthy tasks, but they lead to the downplaying of family and social factors and of ongoing care. Even the name 'after-care' implies that it is something added on, after the main care in hospital has taken place. So the effort is not 'out there', where the patients are living; the effort from the staff is in the hospital. So we find that admissions and readmissions and bed-days in hospital remain high in this form of 'community psychiatry'.

Not infrequently, psychiatrists ask what is wrong with the patient having a brief admission. There are a number of things wrong with it. First of all, patients do not like hospital; they keep telling us that. Secondly, once a person is admitted, it creates ideas in people's minds – for the average citizen, a mental patient is someone who has been to a mental hospital. Thirdly, patients come to realise that their behaviour is labelled as 'mad' and that they are not going to be held responsible for it. Fourthly, relatives come to misidentify the patient's bad behaviour as illness and seek admission for it; this does not solve the problem, because the patient improves in hospital, the bad behaviour stops, the patient comes out, and the process starts again. Fifthly, staff and police quickly readmit patients who have been previously admitted, and there are well known stories of patients turning up at police stations saying that they are from the hospital, and the police taking them back to 'where they belong'.

Another bad thing about hospital admission is that the opportunity to form a close, trusting relationship with a patient and family at the initial interview is lost when a person is admitted. After a brief interview, the decision is made to admit and the doctors can spend time on the case at their convenience. The opportunity to intervene and form the relationship at the time of the crisis is lost.

The quality of life and the quality of care for the mentally ill can be improved. The demonstration projects have proved this and the principles of care used in those projects can be applied in the real world, but we have to persevere to make it happen, and the organisation and structures have to be right to get good results.

References

ANDREWS, G., TEESON, M., STEWART, G., *et al* (1990) Follow up of community placement of the chronic mentally ill in New South Wales. *Hospital and Community Psychiatry*, **41**, 184–188.

HOULT, J. (1986) Community care of the acutely mentally ill. *British Journal of Psychiatry*, **149**, 137–144.

——, REYNOLDS, I., CHARBONNEAU-POWLS, M., *et al* (1983) Psychiatric hospital versus community treatment: the results of a randomised trial. *Australian and New Zealand Journal of Psychiatry*, **17**, 160–169.

REYNOLDS, I., JONES, J., BERRY, D., *et al* (1990) A crisis team for the mentally ill: the effect on patients, relatives and admissions. *Medical Journal of Australia*, **152**, 646–652.

STEIN, L. I. & TEST, M. A. (1980) An alternative to mental hospital treatment. *Archives of General Psychiatry*, **37**, 392–399.

TEST, M. A. & STEIN, L. I. (1978) The clinical rationale for community treatment: a review of the literature. In *Alternatives to Mental Hospital Treatment* (eds L. I. Stein & M. A. Test). New York: Plenum.

WING, J. K., COOPER, J. E. & SARTORIUS, N. (1974) *The Measurement and Classification of Psychiatric Symptoms*. London: Cambridge University Press.

17 A home treatment service in inner-city Birmingham

CHRISTINE DEAN

In central Birmingham the mental illness services are very much divided geographically. I am the consultant responsible for Sparkbrook. We use two health centres and a mental health resource centre.

Sparkbrook is a deprived inner-city electoral ward, with a population of 25 728 (1981 census): 75% of the enumeration districts in the electoral ward are in the worst 2.5% in England and Wales and all are in the worse 10%. According to the Jarman score (Jarman, 1984), which ranges from −62 to +72, it has a score of +62, which puts it in one of the worst ten electoral wards of the 9265 in England and Wales. The population is multiracial, with 35% of heads of households born in the UK, 11% in the Irish Republic, and the remainder in the New Commonwealth, Pakistan, or elsewhere (1981 census). Almost all the population are 'working-class' (social classes III manual, IV or V) and there is much unemployment. Known patients with chronic or severe psychiatric illness number about 150.

Until the resource centre opened, we set up a day service in a community centre, and out-patient clinics in two health centres. We built up our staffing through funding obtained from the Department of Health and Social Security and the transfer of resources from the closure of a ward at the Midland Nerve Hospital (made possible because we had managed to reduce admissions). In our resource centre, the manager is a social worker, and the deputy manager is a National Health Service charge nurse. Roles are flexible and we do whatever is necessary to provide the service. Half the home-treatment team speak Asian languages, because we regard it as essential for patients who are acutely ill to be assessed in their own language. The resource centre provides a total service for the population, except for in-patient care (now needed for very few patients).

Severely ill patients were our priority. All staff do home assessments and we provide a service to the Trinity Night Shelter for the homeless. Referrals are taken from any source. One of the nurses and one of the medical staff assess the patient at home; it is uncommon now to decide that we cannot treat a patient at home. We keep a home treatment record, which includes a medication card, progress notes, and the physical examination sheet; these notes are kept in the patient's house, so that any professional who visits can make a note. So far, we have had few problems with this procedure. Patients who have acute psychiatric illnesses are visited at least daily by the doctors and nurses, but may receive as many as five visits a day. Now that we also have nursing auxiliaries, we are able to place them for several hours at a time in the patient's house, helping the family to manage the patient. This is proving to be very successful. Since October 1988, there has been a nurse on call 24 hours a day. The patients and their relatives have the number of a portable telephone carried by staff and a bleep number which can be called if necessary. At the weekends, there is a nurse on duty on both Saturday and Sunday, and they do the daily visits.

We review the home-treatment patients weekly. As well as the treatment of the acute episode, we work with families and the family members become colleagues in this. This has proved to be very beneficial as a means of encouraging the patient to continue medication; families also alert us immediately if the patient is showing signs of a relapse.

Once the acute episode is over, we provide after-care. Patients who are unable to attend the centre are put on our long-term visiting list. We have started relatives' groups, both for Asian and English-speaking relatives, to give them some education about psychiatric illness.

We treat more Asian patients at home than one would expect from the population figures. This is partly because they dislike coming into hospital (for language and cultural reasons) and partly because they have extended families, who are often more able than their English or Irish neighbours to look after sick relatives at home.

In the first year of the service, 38 patients were treated at home, without admission, while of 54 patients admitted to hospital, only 17 had been assessed by us. With 11 patients, home treatment failed, while it was regarded as unsuitable for six, who had to be admitted. Home treatment patients were more likely to be married than patients who were admitted. Of patients who were admitted, 60% were assessed in hospital; thus, it seems that if the patient reaches hospital, it is difficult to reverse the process at that stage. Quite a high proportion of admissions came from a police station.

Home-treatment patients mainly presented during working hours, whereas 50% of patients who were admitted presented out of hours. Of the home-treatment patients, 29% had had no previous admission, and 45% had been legally committed to hospital in the past; a smaller proportion of the admitted patients had been previously committed to hospital. There are three main diagnoses – mania, depression, and schizophrenia; the depressed patients were usually severely ill. We found no difference in diagnosis between those patients treated at home and those admitted, but relatively more of the admissions were for non-psychotic illnesses – eating disorders, adjustment disorders, and neurotic disorders.

Six patients were regarded by us as unsuitable for home treatment. Three were in police custody, another had a Capgras syndrome, believing that his parents were imposters, and that they were trying to kill him. Another had a fractured tibia and fibula, and the sixth was a suicidal patient with delusional jealousy. Of the 11 patients initially receiving home treatment who had to be admitted, two were women with small children who had manic illnesses accompanied by marked aggression, and two other manic patients had to be admitted because they were aggressive towards their families. Manic patients settle quickly in the community – more so than in hospital – but some depressed patients did not do well. If they were not eating or drinking and would not take medication, they were admitted to hospital. One patient had pathological jealousy, was aggressive to his wife, and had to be admitted. In all, 17 out of the 55 patients we assessed for home treatment that year were admitted, several for systemic medical problems. We increased the range of patients we can treat at home in the second year of our service because of the advent of the 24-hour on-call service for home-treatment patients.

Acknowledgements

I thank Dr Elaine Gadd for her help with the analysis of the data and Dr Stuart Cumella for his provision of the admission statistics.

Reference

JARMAN, B. (1984) Underprivileged areas: validation and distribution of scores. *British Medical Journal*, **289**, 1587–1592.

18 Home treatment and crisis intervention in Lewisham

STEPHEN WOOD

The concept of psychological crisis originated in a study of survivors of a nightclub fire (Lindeman, 1944) and broadened into a theory of reaction to sudden adverse changes (Tyhurst, 1958). Caplan (1961, 1964) developed a model of therapy that exploits the heightened suggestibility and enhanced learning which are thought to occur in crises.

Treatment of acute mental illness has typically been relocated (to district general hospitals) rather than restyled. This chapter describes a service based upon such a model (Stein & Test, 1980; Hobbs, 1984).

The Mental Health Advice Centre

The Mental Health Advice Centre (MHAC) was opened in 1978, in Lewisham, an inner-city area of south-east London. It serves a population of 84 000 – including prosperous Blackheath and an area of deprived older housing (mainly privately rented). Unemployment is above average, and there is growing homelessness. About a fifth of residents are of Afro-Caribbean origin.

The MHAC provides a comprehensive community psychiatric service, including a walk-in service, crisis intervention, and continuing care. Most of the 18 workers are employed by the health authority, but some are seconded by social services, and one from a housing association. There are two consultant psychiatrists and a senior registrar.

Seventy per cent of new clients and 30% of known clients of the multidisciplinary walk-in service are referred by their family doctors (Boardman *et al*, 1987). Thus, it replaces the out-patient clinic. In 1989, there were over 400 attendances, 70% of them new. Forty per cent are allocated to a key worker and receive some form of psychological treatment; the rest are referred to other agencies or to the crisis intervention team. The common diagnoses of 'walk-in' clients are neuroses and adjustment reactions.

TABLE 18.1
Activity of the Crisis Intervention Team in 1988

	No.	%
All referrals	175	100.0
Source of referral		
GP	73	41.7
walk-in service	14	8.0
continuing-care service	32	18.3
social services	17	9.7
client or family	15	8.6
New referrals	89	50.9
Re-referrals	86	49.1
Admitted during course of intervention	51	29.1
Admitted under Mental Health Act 1983	21	12.0

Continuing care is designed for people with psychosis. The key worker co-ordinates the care of a particular client, who is monitored using a computerised case register (National Unit for Psychiatric Research and Development, 1988).

The crisis intervention team (CIT) supplements the walk-in service by rapid domiciliary assessment and management for clients unable or unwilling to visit the centre or found to be acutely ill (Bouras & Tufnell, 1983). It is multidisciplinary and operates during weekday office hours. Newly referred clients are seen at home by two members of the team, and over 80% are assessed on the day of referral. The CIT initiates both immediate treatment and subsequent frequent visits, and gives general practitioners advice and support. The largest single source of referrals to the CIT remains the general practitioner, accounting for 42%. A quarter of referrals concerned clients

TABLE 18.2
Activity of MHAC teams

	Walk-in service[1]	Crisis intervention service[2]	Continuing-care service[3]
Referrals per year	438	175	338
Males: %	37	37	51
Females: %	63	63	49
Aged 16–39 years: %	67	44	25
Aged 40–65 years: %	33	56	75
Employed full or part time: %	57	27	13
Black ethnic groups[4]: %	17	26	27
Diagnosis[5]			
Schizophrenia and paranoid psychoses: %	4	33	48
Affective disorders: %	6	27	35
Neurotic disorders: %	21	29	4

1. Attendances in 1989, other data from Bouras (1982) and Boardman *et al* (1987).
2. Data for 1988.
3. Data for clients registered in December 1989.
4. African, Afro-Caribbean and Asian ethnic groups.
5. Walk-in clients coded according to ICD–9, CIT and continuing-care clients according to ICD–10 and recoded to ICD–9 for this table.

on the continuing-care register, emphasising the vulnerability of this group. The proportion of those suffering from psychoses rose from 39% in 1979–84 to 60% (27% affective disorder, 33% schizophrenia) in 1988. The more likely causes of this increase are the increased numbers discharged from hospital, an 'inner-city' drift of the mentally ill, declining housing stock, high levels of unemployment, and a shift in the policy of the service towards the care of psychosis. Each client receives an average of five visits.

Of all those referred to the CIT in 1988, 29% were admitted to hospital, those at particular risk being females, those living alone, and those suffering from hypomania. A high proportion of admissions (41%) were compulsory. A third of re-referred clients were admitted, compared with a quarter of new referrals, and they were also more than four times more likely to be admitted compulsorily. Table 18.1 gives details of CIT activity during 1988.

Table 18.2 compares the activity of the three MHAC teams.

Conclusions

A comprehensive community psychiatry service must provide home-based acute and emergency care, as well as services for the long-term mentally ill and for clients with neurotic and less severe problems.

Acknowledgements

I am grateful for the help of my colleagues in the CIT, Peter Ashford, Martin Collison, Jan Faizey and Lorraine Reed, and Dr Sue Cope, Consultant Psychiatrist, in preparing this chapter. Mike Sinclair assisted in collection of data.

References

BOARDMAN, A. P., BOURAS, N. & CUNDY, J. (1987) *The Mental Health Advice Centre in Lewisham. Service Usage: Trends from 1978 to 1984.* London: National Unit for Psychiatric Research and Development.

BOURAS, N. (1982) *Mental Health Advice Centre: 3 Years of Experience. Research Report No. 1.* London: Lewisham and North Southwark Health Authority.

—— & TUFNELL, G. (1983) *Mental Health Advice Centre: The Crisis Intervention Team. Research Report No. 2.* London: Lewisham and North Southwark Health Authority.

CAPLAN, G. (1961) *An Approach to Community Mental Health.* New York: Grune & Stratton.

—— (1964) *Principles of Preventive Psychiatry.* New York: Basic Books.

HOBBS, M. (1984) Crisis intervention in theory and practice: a selective review. *British Journal of Medical Psychology*, **57**, 23–34.

LINDEMAN, E. (1944) Symptomatology and management of acute grief. *American Journal of Psychiatry*, **101**, 141.

NATIONAL UNIT FOR PSYCHIATRIC RESEARCH AND DEVELOPMENT (1988) *Towards Co-ordinated Care for People with Long-Term Severe Mental Illness.* London: NUPRD.

STEIN, L. I. & TEST, M. A. (1980) Alternative to mental hospital treatment. I. Conceptual model, treatment program, and clinical evaluation. *Archives of General Psychiatry*, **37**, 392–397.

TYHURST, J. S. (1958) The role of transitional states, including disaster, in mental illness. In *Symposium on Preventive and Social Psychiatry.* Washington, DC: US Government Printing Office.

19 The Daily Living Programme: a controlled study of community care for the severely mentally ill in Camberwell

MATTHIJS MUIJEN, ISAAC M. MARKS and JOSEPH CONNOLLY

The Daily Living Programme (DLP), funded by the Department of Health, started at the Maudsley Hospital in October 1987, with the objective of evaluating whether home care can offer an alternative to hospital care for patients with a serious mental illness (Marks *et al*, 1988). Outcome is measured on the criteria of clinical symptoms, social functioning, family burden, and cost-effectiveness.

Five controlled studies comparing home care with hospital care for the treatment of the seriously mentally ill have been conducted in the US, Canada, and Australia (Braun *et al*, 1981). Significant differences were always reported to be in favour of the home-care groups, which at the end of the study periods showed greater improvements on psychopathology, social functioning, and satisfaction by patient and relatives (Stein & Test, 1980). No study found a superiority of in-patient care on any variable. An additional argument for the value of home care was the loss of acquired gains after patients from the home-care group were returned to standard care, at completion of the project (Stein & Test, 1980).

Method

The DLP is based in South Southwark, a deprived inner-city area. Included in the study were patients aged between 17 and 64 years, suffering from a severe mental illness, who required hospital admission as decided by independent psychiatrists, lived in South Southwark, and did not suffer from a primary addiction or brain damage. Patients who were violent, suicidal, or who presented under a section of the Mental Health Act were accepted. All first admissions and 20% of readmissions were randomised, allowing an evaluation of the efficacy of this form of care for these subgroups. Independent researchers rated patients on entry and after 3, 9, and 18 months. On 1 April 1989, 120 patients had entered the project.

Following randomisation, patients received either standard hospital care or home-based care. If a patient was allocated to the DLP, an assessment was made to decide whether he/she could be cared for at home or whether an initial period of hospital admission was indicated.

DLP care was based on a problem-solving approach, and a case-management model was used. An individual care plan was designed for each patient by the key worker, and this was evaluated regularly. The DLP team consisted of seven nurses, one social worker, one occupational therapist, and one psychiatrist (a senior registrar). After entry into the programme, patients received support as often and for as long as required. Working hours were from 9 a.m. to 5 p.m., seven days a week. Out-of-hours telephone support was always available, and the emergency clinic provided crisis cover at night, although this was very rarely required. The DLP liaised closely with other services in and outside the hospital, accepting responsibility for the co-ordination of care.

Preliminary results

The initial analysis included 60 patients in each treatment group and no differences were found in the distributions of age, sex, or diagnosis.

The group receiving standard treatment used a total of over 4000 hospital days, with an average per patient of 70 days, while DLP patients had been in hospital for a total of just over 800 days – an average of 14 days per patient ($P < 0.001$). Although 80% of DLP patient required admission, 50% stayed in for less than three days, as compared with 5% of the control group. Psychotic patients stayed longer in hospital than neurotic patients in the DLP group, but not in the control group.

DLP patients received an average of two hours of support a week, psychotic patients requiring more care than the neurotic group. At month 18, about 50% of DLP patients continued to need regular follow-up care, for both clinical and social reasons.

Unfortunately, three patients committed suicide and one patient has been charged with murder in the DLP group during the initial two years of the project, but these events did occur a long while after entry into the programme, and they appear to be unrelated to the form of care. One patient in the hospital group died of self-neglect.

A global cost comparison was performed by calculating the cost of days in hospital for both groups, and adding to the community-treatment group the running costs of the DLP. For the total 18 months, no differences in direct treatment costs were found. High DLP starting costs, caused by a full staff complement caring for a slowly increasing number of patients, were compensated for by relative savings in the last six months. During months 12–18, DLP care offered a saving of 25%, suggesting that community care requires an initial investment, but may eventually produce savings.

No analysis has been performed yet of social functioning and family burden, but patients and relatives do prefer DLP care. These data, together with the figures on service use, will provide an indication of the suitability of home care for various groups of patients.

A measure of patient satisfaction was the low drop-out rate of symptomatic patients in the DLP group. Particularly noticeable has been the adherence to follow-up of the young schizophrenic patients, indicating the attraction of a model of care that offers comprehensive support. Many patients were not interested in medical interventions, but requested help with financial, housing, and social problems. After their trust had been gained, compliance with treatment gradually improved.

The co-operation of local-authority departments, on which the DLP often depended for the provision of housing and financial support, was important. The quality of community care depends greatly on the resources available, and the co-ordination of these was an important and time-consuming task.

Although the central role of case management was appreciated by both staff and patients, the burden on the staff was often considerable. The responsibility of care for this group of patients can easily lead to demoralisation and 'burn-out', in the absence of any noticeable improvement. The development of training modules and frequent support of staff needs to be considered as a priority. Without them, programmes such as the DLP are unlikely to succeed.

References

BRAUN, P., KOCHANSKY, G., SHAPIRO, R., *et al* (1981) Overview: deinstitutionalization of psychiatric patients, a critical review of outcome studies. *American Journal of Psychiatry*, **138**, 736–749.

MARKS, I., CONNOLLY, J. & MUIJEN, M. (1988) The Maudsley Daily Living Programme. A controlled cost-effectiveness study of community-based versus standard in-patient care of serious mental illness. *Bulletin of the Royal College of Psychiatrists*, **12**, 22–24.

STEIN, L. & TEST, M. (1980) Alternative to mental hospital treatment: 1. Conceptual model, treatment program and evaluation. *Archives of General Psychiatry*, **37**, 392–397.

20 Family care as an alternative to the mental hospital

IAN R. H. FALLOON and VICTOR GRAHAM-HOLE

Recent research suggests that involving families in stress management may improve clinical disorders, facilitate psychosocial rehabilitation, and enhance the quality of life of the family (Strachan, 1986).

Family care has been considered at best as a poor alternative to hospital care; at worst, it is considered a major 'toxic' factor in the aetiology of some mental disorders. Many services eschew family care and develop alternative support systems, but few of these have been shown to be effective in the long-term management of mental disability. A follow-up study of alternatives to hospital care in the UK suggested that family care was superior to alternatives (Brown *et al*, 1958). Family care is the main support for persons suffering from these conditions (Shepherd *et al*, 1966; Goldberg & Huxley, 1980). In the UK, more than 90% of the professional services for the mentally ill are provided by family practitioners. A very small proportion receive care from hospitals.

We propose that an alternative to a hospital-based service should *support* rather than replace the existing providers of mental health care, leaving the hospital as a resource for specialised intensive assessment and care.

In the absence of adequately controlled research, we are not able to draw firm conclusions about the relative merits of any habitat on the course of disabling psychiatric disorders. It is therefore crucial that the needs of all persons suffering from such disabilities are clearly assessed and continuously monitored, and that persistent efforts are made to meet their needs.

The Buckingham Project began in 1984, five years before opening the hospital-based service; Fig. 20.1 illustrates its basis (Falloon *et al*, 1987). Priority is given to particular goals in terms of the greatest needs, while implementation requires training of staff in state-of-the-art procedures for the treatment of mental disability. Twelve nurses, one psychiatrist, one psychologist, one occupational therapist, one social worker, and two secretaries were recruited for a population of 30 000. These staff were integrated with the four primary-care teams in the North Aylesbury Vale area. An office was provided in each practice and patients were assessed along

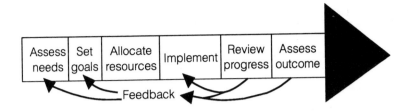

Fig. 20.1. Flow diagram of procedure adopted by the Buckingham Project

with their family members, either in the practice during surgery hours or on home visits. The locus of care was the home, the workplace, the community leisure centre, the community hospital, and the social services, as well as the psychiatric hospital. A concerted effort was made to avoid offering care or treatment that a less specialised person was already providing. Instead, mental health professionals were employed to train, support, and supervise persons in the community to continue to provide care, but in a more effective and efficient manner.

General practitioners have been trained to screen for early signs of psychiatric disorders, and to provide more effective drug therapy as well as some straightforward psychological strategies. The mental health professionals have received training and ongoing supervision in a range of relevant treatment strategies. These have included home-based intensive care (Stein & Test, 1980), anxiety management (Marks, 1987), depression management (Beck *et al*, 1979), and drug and psychosocial care of schizophrenia (Falloon, 1985). Approximately 20% of staff time is spent in training, retraining, and supervision.

Family-based health care is not a new concept. An earlier resident of the Buckingham area, Florence Nightingale, suggested that the best form of health care was to place nursing bonnets on all the family members of a person suffering an illness. Combining drug and psychosocial treatment is effective within a family-based approach in the long-term care of schizophrenia (Strachan, 1986). Families have also been taught stress management and psychosocial rehabilitation procedures, thus reducing clinical morbidity in the patient. The quality of life for patients with schizophrenia and their families is thereby enhanced (Falloon, 1985), and there is evidence for similar benefits from family involvement in affective and anxiety disorders (Mathews *et al*, 1981).

Transferring results obtained from structured research programmes into clinical practice presents a challenge. Our preliminary findings suggest that similar results can indeed be obtained in the field, with reduction in clinical morbidity, enhanced social functioning, reduced family burden, reduced need for continuous drug prophylaxis, low utilisation of intensive care, and consumer and staff satisfaction. It is apparent to us that the needs of the population for mental health services are being met in this way, with very few exceptions. In 1989, a new 22-bed hospital opened in Buckingham. This unit was built from capital for a small mental hospital unit. As a result of the reduced need for in-patient services, it has been designated for the care of all forms of medical disorder in the community, including psychiatric disorders. These benefits are only achieved, however, when a comprehensive team of highly trained mental health professionals is deployed, ensuring that severe psychiatric disorders receive the highest priority, and providing 24-hour intensive care whenever and wherever it is needed.

References

BECK, A. T., RUSH, A. J., SHAW, B. F., *et al* (1979) *Cognitive Therapy of Depression*. New York: Guildford Press.

BROWN, G. W., CARSTAIRS, G. M. & TOPPING, G. C. (1958) Post-hospital adjustment of chronic mental patients. *Lancet*, ii, 685–689.

FALLOON, I. R. H. (1985) *Family Management of Schizophrenia*. Baltimore: Johns Hopkins University Press.

——, WILKINSON, G., BURGESS, J., *et al* (1987) Evaluation in psychiatry: planning, developing and evaluating community-based mental health services for adults. In *Evaluating Mental Health Practice* (ed. D. Milne). London: Croom Helm.

GOLDBERG, D. & HUXLEY, P. (1980) *Mental Illness in the Community: The Pathway to Psychiatric Care*. London: Tavistock Press.

MARKS, I. M. (1987) *Fears, Phobias and Rituals*. New York: Wiley.

MATHEWS, A. M., GELDER, M. G. & JOHNSTON, D. W. (1981) *Agoraphobia: Nature and Treatment*. New York: Guildford Press.

SHEPHERD, M., COOPER, B., BROWN, A. C., *et al* (1966) *Psychiatric Illness in General Practice*. London: Oxford University Press.

STEIN, L. I. & TEST, M. A. (1980) An alternative to mental hospital treatment. *Archives of General Psychiatry*, **37**, 392–399.

STRACHAN, A. M. (1986) Family intervention for the rehabilitation of schizophrenia: toward protection and coping. *Schizophrenia Bulletin*, **12**, 678–698.

IV. Appendix

A debate – "This house recognises the continued need for asylum"

PATRICK G. CAMPBELL, JAMES A. ROBERTSON, JUDY WELEMINSKY and DONALD H. DICK

At the end of the Symposium, a debate was held, chaired by the President of the Royal College of Psychiatrists, Dr James Birley, with Dr Patrick Campbell, Consultant Psychiatrist, Friern Hospital, and Ms Judy Weleminsky, Director of the National Schizophrenia Fellowship, speaking for the motion, and Dr James Robertson, Consultant Psychiatrist, Kidderminster General Hospital, and Dr Donald Dick, Consultant Psychiatrist, Herrison Hospital, speaking against.

The following is a much abridged account of that debate.

Patrick G. Campbell

The shortest letter I have ever received from a general practitioner said, "Dear Doctor, re Mr X, aged 45. Thank you for taking this man in. Yours sincerely". Mr X, when I saw him, was thought-disordered, distressed, deluded, and in a neglected condition; he could not give a coherent account of himself and was being physically restrained by his brother. Fifteen years previously he suffered from a mental illness diagnosed as paranoid schizophrenia. When this became disabling he was admitted to a large mental hospital on a few occasions. After a period of treatment he was discharged recovered and went home to his independent way of life and his work. In more recent years, however, the pattern had changed. Instead of being admitted to the mental hospital, he had gone to the district general hospital (DGH) from which he was discharged unrecovered, because he was said to be too violent. Later he was offered part-time attendance at the day hospital, but was said to be too disturbed to manage there and for a long time had received no treatment at all. The medical records revealed a progressive change in the language doctors used to describe Mr X's behaviour. In the early days, when he went to the mental hospital, he suffered from "terrifying auditory hallucinations". Later, in his days at the DGH unit, it was noted that "he claims to suffer from auditory hallucinations". Later still, at the day hospital, before he was banned from it, the notes recorded that he "likes to tell doctors he hears voices". The district in which he lived had severed its reliance on the mental hospital, and gained some fame for no longer needing such an outmoded resource. Its local social-services department had done away with mental illness as an affliction entitling sufferers to the allocation of a social worker. They had adopted instead the less stigmatising term, 'mental distress'. This story, and I can recount dozens of similar ones, sometimes making me ashamed of my profession, is an allegory of our times, and introduces my proposition that the notion of asylum remains fundamental to the humanitarian treatment of mental disorder. This man had been denied the right of asylum. Some psychiatrists have even been drawn into re-categorising patients' disabilities as purely social or personality problems, terms used to disbar and disown. Often we can find no agreed terms for the person, or the problems we identify, or what we will offer, other than 'care' in that largest and most neglected long-stay ward of all, 'the community'.

An afflicted person should gain – in a humanitarian society – certain rights, such as the right to be assessed as possibly not responsible, in law, for their actions, the right to receive help and treatment and, if necessary, the right to reside somewhere and be cared for, protected from the hostility of uncomprehending people, or perhaps protected from themselves. The person undergoing such disability may recover from it, and society has a duty to assist that process in every way possible.

Some might argue that there is a danger that no person, least of all doctors with their powers to administer reckless physical treatment, can be trusted to carry through such implications in an acceptably humane way, and that we should treat everybody as effectively normal, responsible for their actions and answerable for what they do.

The concept of asylum is as old as European civilisation. It was a privilege granted to people in certain defined places at religious temples. Later, asylum came to be an expression of national sovereignty. A state granted asylum to its citizens and those of other countries – the right not to be seized or extradited. Two main difficulties confront us. The first is whether the concept is distorted and undermined by the possibility of compulsory removal and detention. If you accept, as I do, that some mentally afflicted people need the state to exercise the right of asylum on their behalf, then the detention of people for their own and society's protection does not gainsay the concept of asylum. The other difficulty is whether the concept of asylum for the mentally afflicted has become equated with a particularly awful kind of large Victorian institution for the mentally ill or mentally handicapped. At Friern Hospital, the health advisory service team reported that our buildings were "shockingly unsuited to the practice of modern psychiatry", and they had been condemned in words of that kind since about 1860; but the hospital, with 1500 admissions last year, is now busier than it has ever been. The buildings are old and dilapidated but it is worth noting that a local planning officer suggested that Friern's best use was conversion into luxury flats. It is set in a middle-class area which over 130 years has developed familiarity with, and tolerance for, people with mental illness. Mrs Thatcher, in whose constituency the hospital lies, expressed puzzlement that the hospital should be closing.

Most of the people in the hospital are otherwise homeless and many of them come from the increasing band of mentally ill people disowned by other districts and local authorities. Some organisations claiming to advocate autonomy and respect for users' views appear ready to disown, by terminating their tenancies or banning them from day centres, people whose behaviour is thought unacceptable. Community surveys in my district confirm the increasing numbers of homeless mentally ill people who drift into our inner-city area. The closure of the hospital has become an end in itself.

People say we must pay more attention to users' views, but when patients say they want to stay in Friern, they must not be heeded, even if they have been there for 40 years. The closure of mental hospitals can become a massive diversion, a displacement exercise (in psychoanalytic terms), opening the way for people to believe they are doing something positive.

Asylum is a precious concept whose realisation has often been feeble, overwhelmed by numbers and easily subverted or lost. Our mental hospital embodies the right to sanctuary in a more accepting, knowledgeable and humane way than many still grimmer alternatives available to destitute people with mental illness, particularly those who arrive in central London when they are not wanted elsewhere. I hesitate to see them dispossessed of that right of access to a valuable plot of land in favour or supermarkets and luxury flats.

If better realisations of asylum can be found for those who still require it, I fully support them. But let us not for a moment confuse our difficulties in providing good realisations of the concept of asylum for a lack of need for the concept. To do so I believe threatens to destroy an essential element of the humanitarian approach to mental affliction and disorder.

James A. Robertson

Madness cannot be abolished by relocating it, renaming it, or redefining it as social alienation, political oppression, or an idiosyncratic way of being in the world. Its effects can be modified by treatment but it is seriously distressing and disabling. I agree that there is gross neglect of the needs of such afflicted people, particularly in the large cities but in other settings as well. Such needs include treatment, physical care, social welfare, shelter and, occasionally, custody and control.

Adding to this list of needs, the word 'asylum' introduces another element; the implication of 'asylum' is essentially long-term seclusion for a special group of people in a special setting, remote from and protected from normal society. This idea is superficially seductive but is fundamentally sentimental and ultimately pernicious. It is essentially put forward as a provision that it is good for *someone else* to have. Professor Parry Jones concluded that it was always something imposed on a group who were thought to need it. It is this paternalism that is the fundamental flaw in the concept. It derives partly from 'the pastoral myth' of the mental hospital – that, there, in a green setting, away from the teeming city slum, the 'happy lunatics' are going about their work in the fields or the workshops tended by caring and decent attendants or nurses. The reality has always been different. Any seasoned charge nurse will tell you two things about mental hospitals: the casual acceptance of violence and the casual acceptance of corruption.

Perhaps that is excessively cynical. Perhaps one is only looking at the worst aspects of mental hospital life. But just as important, I think, is the casual acceptance of invalidation; invalidation of the individual's status as an adult, as a citizen, and perhaps even as a human being. Among that sad series of scandals in the 1960s and 1970s, one of the most interesting was that of St Augustine's. St Augustine's was not such a terribly bad mental hospital, and nothing really awful had happened there. The lid was taken off a mental hospital of mediocrity. What was revealed was considered quite unacceptable by modern standards of humane management.

You may say that asylum, as a facility and a concept, does not necessarily imply *an* asylum in the sense of a Victorian hospital. If one accepts implied paternalism, that there are certain people that must be put away by law, with alternatives so difficult they are virtually precluded, this in itself encourages the growth of the old-style institution. Once we accept the need for asylum, the perceived need for it will grow. More and more people will be identified who, in the eyes of others, would be better off tidied away from society. Whenever someone finds that a fellow citizen is difficult and awkward, he is liable to ring our department or the social services, saying that 'this poor soul' needs seclusion in a special sheltered setting: what they really mean is that they are an intolerable nuisance to their neighbours.

If the perceived need for asylum grows, facilities soon become overcrowded and, as with the old hospitals, the needs of the institution, its patterns, practices, timetables and the aspirations of its staff take precedence over the needs of patients. Patients become invisible, having been tidied away from society. Standards in mental hospitals were scandalous for decades but because they were invisible nothing was done about them and it was assumed that people in those places were being looked after satisfactorily. Mental patients in the community retain their status as citizens, but in the asylum they have the status of a lunatic.

The factors that determine how we treat and manage the mentally ill depend on many underlying assumptions, social, legal, and moral. There is a widespread acceptance, which I would endorse, that it is not appropriate to impose on adult citizens restrictions on their liberty unless they have actively endangered the state or others. This is the principle set out in Mill's "Essay on Liberty".

One does not want to punish people with the full weight of the law who have committed infractions while deluded. The Mental Health Act and other legislation, such as the Court of Protection, can take care of that. If we allow asylum (with a small 'a') back in, it is the thin edge of a wedge, the thick end of which is a return to institutions of the type we used to know.

Dr Campbell has asserted that we have failed to address the difference between asylum as a concept and asylum in some more concrete sense. Because asylum as a concept is patronising and overprotective, its realisation in any form is inevitably flawed. The attitude to the asylum patient is that, in transactional-analysis terms, it tends to be very much a parent-to-child transaction. My opponent feels that it is possible to provide sanctuary for mentally ill people in a way which preserves dignity, freedom, autonomy and the possibility of choice. I am deeply sceptical about that. Very few patients at the inception of their illness want such a facility, nor do their relatives. The people who do want continued sanctuary are those who have been there a long time and become dependent on it.

Lucy, a patient I ran across a few years ago, was mildly mentally handicapped, had schizophrenia, was exceptionally miserable, had lost a lot of weight, and had burnt the tip of her nose smoking her cigarettes to the butt. I felt if I had a long-stay ward, she should be in it. A few months later she had met a gentleman with equally unprepossessing social skills and mental state, with a long history of care in Powick Hospital; they got married and set up together in a flat where they have continued to be looked after by community mental health staff, and both are quite contented. Had the asylum facility existed, she would have gone into it and would have lost her niche in normal society, possibly for ever.

Judy Weleminsky

Why have asylums come back into vogue? I cannot say why words seem to be wonderful one day, terrible the next, and wonderful the day after. It may be that once they disappear for a while they come back into fashion, just like clothing.

In the 1985 Short report asylum was defined as the provision of shelter and refuge, and protection from harm and from doing harm. Asylums should be a place of safety, not of custody. They should enhance personal integrity and prevent self-harm.

Claire Baron's book *Asylum to Anarchy* is an interesting examination of anarchy in the community. The anarchy occurred in a psychotherapeutic day centre, and the abuses there were worse than any she had seen in the old mental hospital. Chris Heginbotham (1988) said "a crucial component of asylum is that it is chosen by the users. People seek refuge, not confinement."

Psychiatric disorder is often chronic and intractable and we must face the challenge of providing asylum for such patients. I dream that one day there might be general practitioners who recognise immediately the possibility of serious mental disorder, who immediately refer to a psychiatrist, who welcomes the referral, makes an assessment, preferably in the patient's own home, and listens to the family, who are often much more aware of what the person was like before and what the changed behaviour is all about. If the psychiatrist finds that there is a serious mental disorder he ensures that there is care, support, time, medical and social therapy, life-skills and social-skills training, accommodation, employment, social facilities, finance and all of these for as long as they are needed. It is going to be all the 'Cs' – caring, continuing, co-operative, consistent, comprehensive, and even clear and acceptable. If all that existed, I don't know whether we would need something called 'asylum'.

A booklet produced by the National Schizophrenia Fellowship, *Slipping Through The Net*, is based on a survey of 1988. We produced it because we hear so many horror stories. There was Keith, who was not well and hearing voices. The general practitioner (GP) told him to pull himself together. His mother and fiancee were very worried, so they went to a psychotherapist. He quickly realised that Keith was mentally ill and arranged an appointment with a psychiatrist; but before he saw the psychiatrist he had killed his mother. Mrs M, another mother, noticed that her son was getting worse and for two months begged her GP to do something about it, but the GP had struck him off the list for being too disruptive; so she begged the health authority and the social-services department, and they said they were overstretched. She was beaten up by her son several times and met the officials again. Couldn't a bed be found for him somewhere? A few days later, her son strangled her, and she is now in intensive care. David, 39, lives with his father who is 80, and who can barely cope. David deteriorated and the father took out a summons of restraint, which he did not want to do, so David is now homeless. Alexander was looked after by loving grandparents, and treated by the local hospital, which is now closed; when Alex's condition worsened again, he went back to the hospital, which had given him help and security, found it closed, returned home and lay down on the living-room floor to die. Mr R was put out of hospital; he had no home, attempted suicide, and made repeated attempts to mutilate himself. He had to have 25 stitches in his penis. He was admitted to hospital and sent home again; he mutilated himself again and is now in prison.

Cases like these are the reason why the Fellowship feels so strongly every time the professionals turn somebody away, every time a group home says that a certain person is too difficult, or a hospital says that they have no locked wards anymore, or no staff, or "we know so and so and we don't like them", or the GP says they're too difficult and disruptive. I would like to see asylum with the objectives of maintaining people with illnesses which at the present moment we cannot treat. We need to enable people to leave and to return if they want to, and not to find the doors closed. We need to maintain people in as good a situation as we can. We need to find some way of making asylum a positive experience for patients and staff.

Where asylum is concerned, treatability should not be the criterion. We want a place that will help and care for people even if they are not treatable. Such patients can be protected from harm or from doing harm to others. I am always puzzled by 'personality disorder' – it seems to be a way of saying that nothing more can be done for someone so let's change the diagnosis. It seems to relate to people whom we like to call 'lazy', 'bloody minded', 'difficult', 'disruptive', 'violent', 'unresponsive'. I would like to see asylums which can cope with people who have 'personality disorder'.

I do not want to see asylums that are prisons. We have far too many people in prison already. Dr John Kilgour, Director of the Medical Services of Her Majesty's Prisons, wrote in 1988, "My colleagues and I find ourselves having to handle people who are inappropriately committed to custodial sentences due, to put it bluntly, to the failure of the community to provide suitable facilities for them". Prisons are clearly being used as an alternative to psychiatric care. The consequences of the lack of asylum are terrified, overburdened parents and families, homelessness, personal deterioration, suicide, imprisonment, and 'doss' houses.

I am in favour of asylum, and I urge that in places of asylum we have proper audit to make sure that they are properly run and that they care for and help people, and do not damage them.

Donald H. Dick

I shall call my contribution "courage to think fresh thoughts". I want to make two main points. One is that asylum has not worked and unless we make an assumption that it is not going to continue, we will not be able to invent anything more suitable. Secondly, that arguments against bad community care are not arguments in favour of retaining mental hospitals in their present or an adapted form. Medicine failed and continues to fail many people with chronic mental illness. Should it not invite others to join in the attempt to do something better? One of my successors at the Health Advisory Service, Peter Horricks, says there is no such thing as chronic illness, but there are some patients who die before you have rehabilitated them.

If institutional care was a pill, doctors would stop prescribing it, because it does not work. Then you would think of the alternatives. In most mental hospitals, walking down the corridors or onto the wards, you keep meeting people who, if you were to meet them on the street you would not think "he ought to be in a mental hospital". He seems happy and contented. He has shelter and warmth. He has a social structure. But those are not elements of his treatment. Those are elements of his daily life. Treatment could be separated quite readily from the place where he lives. For the vast majority of the mentally ill, it is necessary to disentangle the place of treatment from the place of living. Why do people need to stay all day in hospital, when they could be equally comfortable somewhere else, and, if necessary, treated there? A mental hospital is, in effect, a large group home or residential home, perhaps a nursing home. There seems no reason why that nursing home should not be in a pleasant part of the town and the people who live there should not use all the facilities that the rest of the citizens do. Of people that you might recognise as being mentally ill, 95% have always lived outside the walls of mental hospital – at home or in domestic surroundings of one sort or another. Only 5% have been in hospitals. As against this, 95% of the mental health professionals are to be found in hospital and 5% outside!

Most psychiatry is not 'high tech'. Most psychiatry is seeing troubled people through difficult times. It is not necessary to bring people long distances from their homes in order to provide that care.

Asylum is a range of places of safekeeping which may be found for people from time to time. I hope we can find a better form of care than that deathless and eternal mental hospital system of 'because you have failed me, I'm going to keep you locked up forever'. Now I do not deny, nor could I, that there are some people who, at times during the course of their mental illness, become a danger to themselves or to others. The question is, is this a permanent state or a temporary state? The great majority of people with mental illness can have those disturbances relieved fairly promptly by the right kind of treatment. Should that person not go back to the life which they had formerly had to abandon? Asylum should be temporary.

Where are the tuberculosis sanitoria? Where did people imagine that people with chronic tuberculosis would be managed? They are being managed, of course, at home.

I was very impressed when I first came to Powick Hospital in 1972. Dr Spencer had had the locks removed from the doors. He had had them unscrewed. This aroused a great deal of anxiety. He had said "now you've got some problems about managing mentally ill people without locked doors". The standard of nursing at Powick Hospital was at that time the best I had seen, because of the problem which Dr Spencer had posed. Nothing will stretch our minds so much as saying we are going to try to do without that place of asylum.

We must remove the asylum from our minds, not just yet, but in the development we pursue. We must assume that people need to be in a safe place from time to time, but we must have this challenge to be inventive, to find better solutions for the 90% who never actually got to mental hospitals, by having the courage to think afresh.

I am not sure that we know yet what that alternative is, and I am not sure that we are ready to abandon what we still have. This must not stop us from looking for a better future alternative.

Judy Weleminsky – closing for the motion

Asylum does not have to be in large, isolated institutions, and 'big' is not necessarily 'bad'. I attended a university with 6000 people. It was a marvellous institution and I enjoyed every minute of it. You can oppress people in many diferent ways, and we could just end up with transinstitutionalisation. We are talking about a multidisciplinary asylum, which involves the families, which involves the community, which involves befriending, which has continual audit and revision of what is being done and how it is being done, and makes it stay alive instead of being forgotten. I think there is plenty of challenge there and instead of putting down this patronising, overprotective institution, let us accept the fact that for some people (not for all) the community can be a very cruel, neglecting and underprotective place.

Donald H. Dick – closing against the motion

I wish I did not have to speak again because I was very much more certain in trying to look at the hypothesis that we can do without asylum at the beginning than I am now. It is possible to see a number of futures without asylum as we have understood it. It is equally possible that we can see futures in which there is asylum within the system. Many dreadful institutions are still going strong. There are some extraordinarily dangerous people who can never, alas, walk abroad again. But that does not mean to say that, in addition to being deprived of their freedom, very often through no fault of their own, they should have an oppressed life. There is a distinction – asylum as prison and asylum as a place of rest. I stick to the point that if we do not intellectually discard the need for asylum during this phase of opportunity for change in our systems, we will not think of a better alternative than we have at the moment. We will, it seems, inevitably slip back to the mindless outcome of locking the door and saying 'there, the problem is solved'.

The motion was put to the house and carried.

Index

Compiled by Stanley Thorley